GREATFASTRECIPES

GREATFASTRECIPES

THE AUSTRALIAN
Women's Weekly

contents

fast food

Quick and easy – that's what we want when it comes time to cook. Our busy lives leave us little time for fiddling around with long, complicated recipes. Whether you want a quick snack or something more substantial, *Great Fast Recipes* is loaded with no-fuss, nourishing food in a flash – which is also great when it comes to entertaining. So, toss out those boring, old standbys, and add some inspiration to your table. The recipes are fresh, with a modern twist, and all can be made easily on the night, so you can spend more time with family and friends and less in the kitchen. There are more than 190 recipes to choose from, and many can be on the table in 30 minutes.

Make the most of your freezer

- Freezer containers must be airtight, so food does not dry out, discolour or develop off-flavours.
- Shallow containers are best for freezing because food freezes and thaws more quickly if packed in thin layers.
- Freeze fresh herbs, chillies, lemon grass and ginger either dry, in freezer bags, or finely chopped, in ice-cube trays, barely covered with water. Once frozen, transfer herbs to freezer bags for storage. Wash and dry the herbs well first; peel the ginger, but freeze in pieces.
- Freeze citrus juice or stock in ice-cube bags (available from supermarkets) or trays, then add one or two cubes, as required, to sauces, soups, etc.
- Leftover rice and cooked dried (not fresh) pasta freezes very well.
- If not defrosting with a microwave, frozen food should be thawed in the refrigerator (allow 10 to 24 hours to thaw, depending on the quantity of food).

Get to know your microwave

- Your microwave has other uses than just rewarming or defrosting, and can cut down both the preparation and cooking time.
- Smaller pieces of food cook faster than large ones, so cut all your ingredients into similar-sized pieces to ensure even cooking.
- Cook food in batches, as overloading your microwave will increase cooking time and the food may not cook evenly.
- It's better to undercook food slightly, then increase cooking time until the food is cooked as desired. Don't forget standing time, as most food continues cooking after being removed from the microwave.
- If cooking foods of uneven thickness, the thickest part should be positioned facing the walls of the microwave.
- It's important to stir or reposition food during the cooking, as microwaves, as a rule, do not cook evenly.

Quick tips

- Before you do your weekly shop, plan your weekly menu. Work out what you're going to eat, and buy all your dry and canned ingredients. Fresh ingredients can be bought as you need them.
- If you can't plan your weekly menu, a well-stocked pantry, refrigerator and freezer can be a lifesaver, ensuring there is always food on standby to create a meal.
- Invest in a wok, and you can create delicious stir-fries in minutes.
- One of the best ways to save time in the kitchen is to cook twice as much as you need and, where appropriate, freeze the rest, or take it for lunch later in the week.
- Sauces can be cooked and refrigerated or frozen; meat and fish can be marinated overnight, ready to stir-fry the next evening.
- Buy tender, choice cuts of meat. These may seem extravagant at first, but if time is your priority, you'll save plenty with these quick-cooking meats.
- Eat more fish. Not only does it cook very fast, it's also full of omega-3 fats, necessary for a healthy heart.
- Fast-cooking chicken fillets are ideal for a healthy time-saving meal, and using pre-cooked barbecue chicken saves even more time.
- One of the quickest-cooking ingredients is pasta, and fresh pasta cooks in even less time. Noodles often only need to be refreshed under hot water.
- Keep good-quality bottled sauces on hand; these are great time-savers.
- Use bottled crushed garlic, minced ginger, lemon grass, chopped chillies, herbs, etc.

seafood

Salmon with lime and chilli sauce, crab salad or prawn risotto, seafood is the freshest of all ingredients and the fastest to cook. Most fishmongers will prepare your seafood, saving you even more time in the kitchen. Take advantage of its bountiful supply and health benefits.

blue-eye cutlets with pesto butter

PREPARATION TIME 10 MINUTES COOKING TIME 10 MINUTES

80g butter
2 tablespoons basil pesto
¼ teaspoon cracked
  black pepper
1 teaspoon finely grated
  lemon rind
4 blue-eye cutlets (800g)
100g baby spinach leaves,
  trimmed

1 Blend or process butter, pesto, pepper and rind in small bowl until well combined.
2 Cook fish, in batches, in large heated lightly oiled non-stick frying pan until browned both sides and cooked as desired.
3 Place butter mixture in same pan; stir over low heat until butter melts. Return fish to pan; coat with melted butter mixture.
4 Serve fish with baby spinach leaves.

serves 4
per serving 24.5g fat; 1584kJ (379 cal)
tip There are many versions of basil pesto you can buy – some are sold fresh, under refrigeration, while others are available bottled on supermarket shelves. Experiment until you find one you like best.

salmon with lime and chilli sauce

PREPARATION TIME 10 MINUTES COOKING TIME 10 MINUTES

2 cloves garlic, crushed
1 teaspoon grated lime rind
1cm piece fresh ginger (5g),
  grated finely
4 salmon fillets (880g)
20g butter
1 tablespoon peanut oil
8 baby bok choy, halved
¹/₃ cup (80ml) sweet chilli sauce
¼ cup (60ml) lime juice
2 tablespoons chopped
  fresh coriander

1 Rub half of the combined garlic, rind and ginger over the flesh side of the salmon.
2 Heat butter and oil in large frying pan until the butter begins to foam. Add salmon, cook until browned on both sides and cooked as desired. Salmon is best served medium rare. Remove salmon from pan, cover to keep warm.
3 Add bok choy to same pan with remaining garlic mixture, chilli sauce and lime juice; stir until the bok choy is just tender.
4 Sprinkle salmon with coriander and serve with bok choy mixture.

serves 4
per serving 25.6g fat; 1890kJ (452 cal)

fish fillets pan-fried with pancetta and caper herb butter

PREPARATION TIME 15 MINUTES   COOKING TIME 10 MINUTES

80g butter, softened
2 tablespoons coarsely chopped fresh flat-leaf parsley
1 tablespoon capers, rinsed, drained
2 cloves garlic, quartered
2 green onions, chopped coarsely
8 slices pancetta (120g)
4 white fish fillets (800g)
1 tablespoon olive oil
350g asparagus, trimmed

1 Blend or process butter, parsley, capers, garlic and onion until mixture forms a smooth paste.
2 Spread 1 heaped tablespoon of butter mixture on each fish fillet, top with two slices of pancetta.
3 Heat oil in large heavy-based frying pan; cook fish, pancetta-butter side down, until pancetta is crisp. Turn fish carefully; cook, uncovered, until cooked as desired.
4 Meanwhile, boil, steam or microwave asparagus until tender.
5 Serve fish and asparagus drizzled with pan juices.

serves 4
per serving 29.6g fat; 1965kJ (469 cal)

fish with wasabi mayonnaise

PREPARATION TIME 5 MINUTES COOKING TIME 10 MINUTES

Wasabi, japanese horseradish, is available as a paste in tubes or powdered in tins from Asian food stores and some supermarkets.

$1/3$ **cup (100g) mayonnaise**
2 teaspoons wasabi paste
2 green onions, chopped finely
**2 tablespoons coarsely chopped
   fresh coriander**
2 tablespoons lime juice
1 tablespoon peanut oil
4 firm white fish fillets (800g)
500g chinese broccoli

1 Combine mayonnaise, wasabi, onion, coriander and juice in small bowl; cover.
2 Heat oil in large frying pan; cook fish, in batches, until browned both sides and cooked as desired.
3 Meanwhile, boil, steam or microwave chinese broccoli until just tender; drain. Divide among serving plates; top with fish and wasabi mayonnaise.

serves 4
per serving 17.2g fat; 1505kJ (359 cal)
tip For a stronger, more fiery taste, add an extra teaspoon of wasabi to the mayonnaise mixture.

fish with basil and black olives

PREPARATION TIME 10 MINUTES   COOKING TIME 10 MINUTES

This recipe is best made close to serving. Blue eye, perch and ling fillets would be suitable.

1 tablespoon extra virgin olive oil
4 white fish fillets (800g)
750g spinach, trimmed,
   chopped coarsely
1 tablespoon lemon juice
¼ teaspoon dried chilli flakes
⅓ cup (80ml) extra virgin
   olive oil, extra
1 clove garlic, crushed
⅓ cup (50g) kalamata olives
¼ cup finely shredded fresh basil

1 Heat oil in large non-stick frying pan, add fish and cook until browned both sides and just cooked through.
2 Meanwhile, boil, steam or microwave spinach until just tender; drain.
3 Combine lemon juice, chilli, extra oil, garlic, olives and basil in the fish pan, cook, stirring, until hot.
4 Serve spinach topped with fish and drizzled with oil mixture.

serves 4
per serving 27.9g fat; 1878kJ (449 cal)

thai fish parcels

PREPARATION TIME 10 MINUTES   COOKING TIME 15 MINUTES

If you can't buy kaffir lime leaves, substitute the young leaves from any other citrus tree.

200g rice stick noodles
4 bream fillets (600g)
150g baby bok choy, quartered
150g snow peas, sliced thinly lengthways
1 tablespoon thinly sliced lemon grass
8 kaffir lime leaves, torn
1 teaspoon soy sauce
2 tablespoons sweet chilli sauce
1 teaspoon fish sauce
2 tablespoons lime juice
1 tablespoon coarsely chopped fresh coriander

1   Preheat oven to hot.
2   Place noodles in large heatproof bowl; cover with boiling water. Stand until just tender; drain.
3   Divide noodles into four equal portions; place each on a large piece of foil. Top noodles with fish; top fish with equal amounts of bok choy, snow peas, lemon grass and lime leaves. Drizzle with combined sauces and juice. Enclose fish stacks in foil; place in single layer on oven tray.
4   Cook fish stacks in hot oven 15 minutes or until fish is cooked through; open foil and transfer stacks to serving plates. Sprinkle with coriander.

serves 4
per serving   4.4g fat; 1393kJ (333 cal)
tip   Fish parcels can be assembled several hours ahead; store in refrigerator.

cajun blue-eye cutlets with lime

PREPARATION TIME 5 MINUTES   COOKING TIME 10 MINUTES

*Cajun cooking, originating in Louisiana, is a blend of French, African and indigenous American styles
used to prepare the seafood and vegetables native to the sultry region of the southern United States.*

2 teaspoons ground cumin
2 teaspoons ground coriander
2 teaspoons sweet paprika
2 teaspoons mustard powder
2 teaspoons onion powder
$^1/_2$ teaspoon garlic powder
$^1/_4$ teaspoon cayenne pepper
2 teaspoons fennel seeds
4 blue-eye cutlets (800g)
2 limes, sliced thickly

1 Combine spices, powders, pepper and seeds with fish in large bowl. Coat fish all over in spice mixture; cook fish on heated oiled grill plate (or grill or barbecue) until browned both sides and cooked as desired.

2 Meanwhile, cook lime on heated oiled grill plate until browned both sides.

3 Serve fish topped with lime slices.

serves 4
per serving 4.4g fat; 854kJ (204 cal)
tips Any firm white fish, such as ling, can be used instead of the blue-eye. You can use $^1/_3$ cup bottled cajun spice mix, available from supermarkets, instead of making your own, if preferred.

prawn and mint salad

PREPARATION TIME 30 MINUTES

1kg medium cooked prawns
1 lebanese cucumber (130g)
1 tablespoon fish sauce
¹/₄ cup (60ml) lime juice
¹/₂ cup (125ml) coconut milk
2 tablespoons sugar
1 clove garlic, crushed
2cm piece fresh ginger (10g),
    grated finely
1 small fresh red thai chilli,
    sliced finely
3 cups snow pea tendrils (60g)
3 cups watercress (60g)
2 cups bean sprouts (160g)
¹/₂ cup thinly sliced fresh mint

1   Shell and devein prawns, leaving tails intact. Halve cucumber lengthways, slice thinly on the diagonal.
2   Whisk sauce, juice, milk, sugar, garlic, ginger and chilli in large bowl until well combined; add prawns, cucumber and remaining ingredients, toss salad gently to combine.

serves 4
per serve 9.8g fat; 1554kJ (371 cal)

mustard-seed chilli prawns

PREPARATION TIME 20 MINUTES COOKING TIME 7 MINUTES

Mustard seeds are available in black, brown or yellow varieties; here, we used black, as they are more spicy and piquant than the other varieties. You can purchase mustard seeds from major supermarkets or health food shops.

1kg large uncooked prawns
$1/4$ teaspoon ground turmeric
2 small fresh red thai chillies, seeded, chopped finely
2 tablespoons vegetable oil
2 teaspoons black mustard seeds
2 cloves garlic, crushed
2 tablespoons finely chopped fresh coriander

1 Shell and devein prawns, leaving tails intact. Cut along back of prawn, taking care not to cut all the way through; flatten prawn slightly.
2 Rub turmeric and chilli into prawns in medium bowl.
3 Heat oil in large frying pan; cook mustard seeds and garlic, stirring, until seeds start to pop. Add prawn mixture; cook, stirring, until prawns just change colour. Stir in coriander.

serves 4
per serving 10.1g fat; 823kJ (197 cal)
tip If you like hot dishes, don't seed the chillies before chopping, as removing the seeds and membranes lessens the heat level.
serving suggestion Garnish with spring onion curls.

crisp-skinned snapper with stir-fried vegetables and black beans

PREPARATION TIME 15 MINUTES COOKING TIME 10 MINUTES

½ teaspoon sea salt

1 teaspoon coarsely ground
    black pepper

4 snapper fillets (1kg)

1 teaspoon sesame oil

1 large brown onion (200g),
    cut into thin wedges

1 clove garlic, crushed

1cm piece fresh ginger (5g),
    grated finely

1 tablespoon salted black beans,
    rinsed, drained

1 medium green capsicum (200g),
    chopped coarsely

1 medium red capsicum (200g),
    chopped coarsely

6 green onions, sliced thickly

100g snow peas

100g broccolini, chopped coarsely

½ cup (125ml) water

¼ cup (60ml) oyster sauce

2 tablespoons lemon juice

500g baby bok choy, chopped coarsely

1 cup bean sprouts (80g)

1 Combine salt and pepper in small bowl; rub into skin side of each fillet. Cook fish, skin-side down, on heated lightly oiled grill plate (or grill or barbecue) until browned and crisp; turn, cook until browned and cooked as desired. Cover to keep warm.

2 Heat oil in wok or large frying pan; stir-fry brown onion, garlic and ginger until onion softens. Add beans; stir-fry 1 minute. Add capsicums, green onion, snow peas and broccolini; stir-fry until vegetables are just tender.

3 Stir in the water, sauce and juice; cook, stirring, until mixture thickens slightly. Add bok choy and bean sprouts; stir-fry until heated through.

4 Serve fish on vegetables.

serves 4
per serving 5.9g fat; 1406kJ (336 cal)
tip Broccolini, a cross between broccoli and chinese kale, is milder and sweeter than broccoli. Each long stem is topped by a loose floret that closely resembles broccoli; from floret to stem, broccolini is completely edible. Substitute chinese broccoli (gai larn) for the broccolini in this recipe, if you prefer.

prawns with hot spicy pesto

PREPARATION TIME 25 MINUTES COOKING TIME 15 MINUTES

1kg uncooked king prawns
2 medium white onions (300g)
2 tablespoons peanut oil
3 cups bean sprouts (240g)

HOT SPICY PESTO
¼ cup finely chopped fresh basil
2 tablespoons finely chopped
** fresh coriander**
¼ cup (60ml) peanut oil
2 teaspoons sambal oelek
4 cloves garlic, crushed
1cm piece fresh ginger (5g),
** grated finely**
2 tablespoons dry sherry
1 teaspoon sesame oil

1 Shell and devein prawns, leaving tails intact. Combine prawns and hot spicy pesto in large bowl. Cut onions into wedges.

2 Heat oil in wok or large frying pan; stir-fry onion until just tender. Stir in prawn mixture; stir-fry until prawns are tender. Add bean sprouts.

hot spicy pesto Blend or process ingredients until smooth.

serves 4
per serving 25.7g fat; 2025kJ (484 cal)
tip Pesto can be made up to three days ahead and refrigerated, covered.

chilli tuna pasta salad

PREPARATION TIME 15 MINUTES COOKING TIME 15 MINUTES

300g large shell pasta
250g fresh green beans, trimmed, halved
2 x 185g cans tuna in chilli oil
¹/₃ cup coarsely chopped fresh flat-leaf parsley
¹/₃ cup firmly packed fresh basil leaves, torn
2 tablespoons baby capers, rinsed, drained
150g baby rocket leaves
¹/₄ cup (60ml) olive oil
¹/₄ cup (60ml) lemon juice
2 cloves garlic, crushed
2 teaspoons sugar

1 Cook pasta in large saucepan of boiling water, uncovered, until just tender; drain. Rinse under cold water; drain.

2 Meanwhile, boil, steam or microwave beans until just tender; drain. Rinse under cold water; drain.

3 Drain tuna; reserve oil. Place tuna in large bowl; flake with fork. Add pasta and beans with herbs, capers and rocket; toss gently to combine.

4 Place remaining ingredients and reserved oil in screw-topped jar; shake well. Drizzle dressing over salad; toss gently to combine.

serves 6
per serving 24.3g fat; 1890kJ (452 cal)
tip The salad, without the dressing, can be made several hours ahead and refrigerated, covered. Toss the dressing through the salad just before serving.

fish in spicy coconut cream

PREPARATION TIME 15 MINUTES   COOKING TIME 20 MINUTES

2 teaspoons peanut oil
2 cloves garlic, crushed
1cm piece fresh ginger (5g),
   grated finely
20g piece fresh turmeric, grated finely
2 small fresh red thai chillies,
   sliced thinly
1½ cups (375ml) fish stock
400ml can coconut cream
20g piece fresh galangal, halved
1 stick fresh lemon grass,
   cut into 2cm pieces
4 firm white fish fillets (800g)
2 tablespoons fish sauce
2 green onions, sliced thinly

1 Heat oil in wok or large frying pan; cook garlic, ginger, turmeric and chilli, stirring, until fragrant. Add stock, coconut cream, galangal and lemon grass; bring to a boil. Add fish, reduce heat; simmer, covered, about 8 minutes or until fish is cooked as desired. Remove and discard galangal and lemon grass pieces.

2 Using slotted spoon, remove fish carefully from sauce; place in serving bowl, cover to keep warm. Bring sauce to a boil; boil 5 minutes. Remove from heat; stir in fish sauce and onion. Pour sauce over fish in bowl.

serves 4
per serving   24.5g fat; 1735kJ (414 cal)
tip   Wear kitchen gloves while grating the turmeric to avoid turning your fingers yellow.

stir-fried seafood with asian greens

PREPARATION TIME 20 MINUTES COOKING TIME 20 MINUTES

You can use flathead, snapper, ling, bream or any other firm white fish in this recipe.

500g medium uncooked prawns
500g squid hoods
500g firm white fish fillets
1 tablespoon peanut oil
5 green onions, chopped coarsely
2 cloves garlic, sliced thinly
10cm piece fresh ginger (50g),
    peeled, sliced thinly
500g baby bok choy, trimmed,
    chopped coarsely
500g choy sum, trimmed,
    chopped coarsely
2 tablespoons light soy sauce
2 tablespoons oyster sauce
1 tablespoon mild chilli sauce

1 Shell and devein prawns, leaving tails intact. Cut squid hoods in half. Score inside surface of each piece; cut into 5cm-wide strips. Cut fish into 3cm pieces.
2 Heat half of the oil in wok or large frying pan; stir-fry seafood, in batches, until browned all over and cooked through.
3 Heat remaining oil in wok; stir-fry onion, garlic and ginger until onion softens.
4 Return seafood to wok. Add bok choy, choy sum and combined sauces; stir-fry until greens are just wilted and heated through.

serves 4
per serving 9.9g fat; 1531kJ (366 cal)

grilled octopus salad

PREPARATION TIME 15 MINUTES COOKING TIME 5 MINUTES

$^{1}/_{3}$ **cup (80ml) orange juice**
1 tablespoon lemon juice
$^{2}/_{3}$ **cup (160ml) olive oil**
1 clove garlic, crushed
600g cleaned baby octopus
1 cup (150g) seeded kalamata olives
5 lebanese cucumbers (650g), seeded, chopped coarsely
200g grape tomatoes, halved
$^{1}/_{3}$ **cup coarsely chopped fresh flat-leaf parsley**

1   Combine juices, oil and garlic in screw-top jar; shake well.
2   Cook octopus, in batches, on heated oiled grill plate (or grill or barbecue) until browned lightly and tender.
3   Toss octopus and dressing in medium bowl; add olives, cucumber, tomato and parsley. Toss gently to combine.

serves 4
per serving 39.6g fat; 2368kJ (566 cal)
tip Grape tomatoes are a newcomer to the tomato tray, and are so delicious they're worth seeking out. However, if you can't find them, substitute cherry tomatoes.

microwave prawn and pea risotto

PREPARATION TIME 5 MINUTES COOKING TIME 25 MINUTES

600g cooked large prawns
20g butter
1 small leek (200g), sliced thinly
2 cloves garlic, crushed
8 saffron threads
2 cups (400g) arborio rice
2 cups (500ml) boiling water
1 cup (250ml) dry white wine
1½ cups (375ml) fish stock
1 cup (120g) frozen peas
2 tablespoons coarsely chopped
**   fresh chives**
¼ cup (60ml) lemon juice
30g butter, extra

1 Shell and devein prawns, leaving tails intact.
2 Place butter, leek, garlic and saffron in large microwave-safe bowl; cook in microwave oven on HIGH (100%), covered, about 2 minutes or until leek softens. Stir in rice; cook on HIGH (100%), covered, 1 minute. Add the water, wine and stock; cook on HIGH (100%), covered, 15 minutes, pausing to stir three times during cooking.
3 Add peas and prawns (reserve a few for garnish, if desired); cook on HIGH (100%), covered, 3 minutes. Stir in chives, juice and extra butter.

serves 4
per serving 12.2g fat; 2574kJ (615 cal)

stir-fried octopus with thai basil

PREPARATION TIME 20 MINUTES COOKING TIME 10 MINUTES

1kg baby octopus
2 teaspoons peanut oil
2 teaspoons sesame oil
2 cloves garlic, crushed
2 small fresh red thai chillies,
  sliced thinly
2 large red capsicums (700g),
  sliced thinly
6 green onions, cut into 2cm lengths
¼ cup firmly packed fresh
  thai basil leaves
¼ cup (60ml) fish sauce
¼ cup (65g) grated palm sugar
1 tablespoon kecap manis

1 Remove and discard the head and beak of each octopus; cut each octopus in half. Rinse under cold water; drain.

2 Heat peanut oil in wok or large frying pan; stir-fry octopus, in batches, until browned all over and tender. Cover to keep warm.

3 Heat sesame oil in wok; stir-fry garlic, chilli and capsicum until capsicum is just tender. Return octopus to wok with remaining ingredients; stir-fry until basil leaves wilt and sugar dissolves.

serves 4
per serving 6.4g fat; 1048kJ (250 cal)

crab salad

PREPARATION TIME 15 MINUTES

500g fresh crab meat
250g chinese cabbage, chopped finely
1 lebanese cucumber (130g), seeded, chopped coarsely
1 medium red onion (170g), halved, sliced thinly
6 green onions, cut into 4cm lengths
1 cup loosely packed fresh thai mint leaves

DRESSING
2 cloves garlic, crushed
2 tablespoons lime juice
2 tablespoons fish sauce
1 tablespoon brown sugar
2 small fresh red thai chillies, chopped finely

1 Drain crab in strainer; remove any shell and, if necessary, shred the meat to desired texture.
2 Combine crab in large bowl with cabbage, cucumber, onions and mint; pour in dressing, toss to combine.
   dressing Combine ingredients in screw-top jar; shake well.

serves 4
per serving 1g fat; 529kJ (126 cal)

tunisian tuna salad

PREPARATION TIME 30 MINUTES COOKING TIME 2 MINUTES

2 hard-boiled eggs

1 medium green capsicum (200g),
    chopped finely

2 medium tomatoes (300g), seeded,
    chopped finely

4 green onions, chopped finely

2 large canned anchovy fillets,
    drained, chopped finely

10 seeded green olives (30g),
    chopped finely

2 small fresh red thai chillies,
    seeded, chopped finely

2 teaspoons finely chopped fresh mint

185g can tuna, drained, flaked

1 tablespoon baby capers,
    rinsed, drained

HARISSA-STYLE DRESSING

2 tablespoons olive oil

1 clove garlic, crushed

1 teaspoon coriander seeds

1 teaspoon caraway seeds

1 tablespoon lemon juice

2 tablespoons red wine vinegar

1 Shell hard-boiled eggs; chop finely.

2 Combine egg with remaining ingredients in medium bowl; drizzle dressing over salad, toss gently to combine.

harissa-style dressing Heat oil in small frying pan, add garlic and seeds; cook, stirring, until fragrant. Stir in juice and vinegar.

serves 4

per serve 14.2g fat; 995kJ (238 cal)

tips You can omit the canned tuna and serve the salad with fresh char-grilled tuna.

This colourful salad from the Tunisian capital of Tunis tastes as good as it looks. North Africans like their food highly spiced and, while this recipe includes only two chillies, you can increase or decrease the quantity as you like.

mussel broth with black bean sauce

PREPARATION TIME 20 MINUTES COOKING TIME 25 MINUTES

1 cup (200g) jasmine rice
1kg small black mussels
1 cup (250ml) water
¹/₃ cup (80ml) black bean sauce
**2 large fresh red chillies, seeded,
   sliced thinly**
4 green onions, sliced thinly

1 Add rice to large saucepan of boiling water; boil, uncovered, until just tender; drain.
2 Meanwhile, scrub mussels; remove beards. Place the water, black bean sauce and chilli in large saucepan; bring to the boil.
3 Add mussels, cook, covered, about 3 minutes or until mussels open (discard any that remain closed).
4 Divide rice among serving bowls; top with mussels and broth. Sprinkle with green onion.

serves 4
per serving 5g fat; 1685kJ (403 cal)

pawpaw, pineapple and mint juice

Blend or process peeled and chopped fresh pawpaw, oranges, limes and pineapple until smooth. Stir in sliced fresh mint.

peach smoothie

Blend or process soy milk with a pinch of ground cinnamon, a peeled and chopped fresh banana and a peach until smooth.

pancetta egg cups

Line base and sides of muffin pan with pancetta, overlapping to form cup shape. Sprinkle with chopped green onions, then break an egg into each pancetta cup. Bake in moderately hot oven about 10 minutes or until eggs are just cooked; serve with toast, sprinkle with sliced green onion.

chocolate hazelnut croissants

Cut ready-rolled puff pastry sheet into four triangles. Spread with Nutella, leaving a 1cm border; sprinkle with grated dark chocolate. Roll triangles, starting at the wide end; place on greased oven tray with tip tucked under and shaped in a crescent. Brush with melted butter. Bake in hot oven 12 minutes, serve dusted with icing sugar mixture.

mixed melon and strawberry juice

Blend or process peeled and chopped fresh honeydew melon, watermelon and strawberries until smooth.

morning trifle

In tall clear individual glasses, layer your favourite breakfast cereal with vanilla yogurt and fresh fruit.

grilled mango and ricotta with english muffins

Spread toasted english muffins with ricotta cheese, top with grilled mango cheeks, drizzle with honey, sprinkle with ground nutmeg.

fruit compote with honey yogurt

Combine orange juice, water, honey and a cinnamon stick in saucepan; bring to the boil. Add dried pears, apricots and fresh dates; simmer about 5 minutes or until fruit is soft. Remove cinnamon stick before serving; serve warm fruit with honey yogurt.

poultry

The perfect fast food – this multipurpose meat is easy to prepare and can be cooked in a variety of ways, from the fastest of stir-fries to the healthiest of salads. Sticky barbecue wings, thai green chicken curry or chicken salsa wraps are just some of the recipes that can be on your table in a flash.

chicken and lime noodle salad

PREPARATION TIME 10 MINUTES

This noodle salad is fast, fresh and full of flavour. Bean thread noodles, also known as vermicelli, mung bean or green bean noodles, are available from Asian food stores and some supermarkets. You need to purchase a large barbecued chicken weighing approximately 900g for this recipe.

200g bean thread noodles
1 medium carrot (120g), sliced thinly
2 green onions, sliced thinly
1 medium red capsicum (200g), sliced thinly
2$^1/_2$ cups (400g) shredded cooked chicken
$^1/_2$ cup loosely packed fresh mint leaves
$^1/_2$ cup coarsely chopped fresh coriander
2 cloves garlic, crushed
1 small fresh red thai chilli, seeded, chopped finely
2 tablespoons rice vinegar
$^1/_2$ cup (125ml) lime juice
$^1/_3$ cup (80ml) peanut oil
2 tablespoons fish sauce

1 Place noodles in large heatproof bowl; cover with boiling water. Stand until just tender; drain.
2 Combine noodles in large bowl with carrot, onion, capsicum, chicken, herbs and combined remaining ingredients; toss gently to combine.

serves 6
per serving 26.9g fat; 1571kJ (376 cal)
tips Noodles can be soaked and drained several hours ahead; refrigerate, covered, until you're ready to assemble the salad.
If you remove the skin from the barbecued chicken before use, you can reduce the fat content of this salad.

honey chilli chicken salad

PREPARATION TIME 15 MINUTES COOKING TIME 10 MINUTES

You will need about two bunches of asparagus and a quarter of a medium chinese cabbage for this recipe.

500g chicken breast fillets, sliced thinly
¼ cup (90g) honey
4 small fresh red thai chillies, seeded,
    sliced thinly
4cm piece fresh ginger (20g),
    grated finely
500g asparagus, trimmed
2 tablespoons peanut oil
4 green onions, sliced thinly
1 medium green capsicum (200g),
    sliced thinly
1 medium yellow capsicum (200g),
    sliced thinly
1 medium carrot (120g), sliced thinly
150g chinese cabbage, shredded finely
⅓ cup (80ml) lime juice

1 Combine chicken, honey, chilli and ginger in medium bowl.
2 Cut asparagus spears in half; boil, steam or microwave until just tender. Rinse immediately under cold water; drain.
3 Meanwhile, heat half of the oil in wok or large frying pan; stir-fry chicken, in batches, until browned all over and cooked through.
4 Place chicken and asparagus in large bowl with onion, capsicums, carrot, cabbage, juice and remaining oil; toss gently to combine.

serves 4
per serving 20.9g fat; 1704kJ (408 cal)
tip A barbecued chicken also can be used; remove and discard bones and skin, then shred meat coarsely before tossing with remaining salad ingredients.

chicken, fennel and orange salad

PREPARATION TIME 15 MINUTES COOKING TIME 10 MINUTES

1 tablespoon olive oil
30g butter
500g chicken breast fillets, sliced thinly
1 large fennel bulb (550g), sliced thinly
¹/₂ cup (60g) seeded black olives, quartered
3 green onions, chopped coarsely
2 medium oranges (480g), segmented
80g rocket leaves

DRESSING
¹/₂ cup (125ml) orange juice
2 tablespoons red wine vinegar
2 tablespoons olive oil
¹/₂ teaspoon sugar

1 Heat oil and butter in large frying pan. Cook chicken, stirring, until well browned and tender; drain.

2 Combine chicken, fennel, olives, onion, orange, rocket and dressing in large bowl; toss gently.

dressing Combine ingredients in screw-top jar; shake well.

 serves 4
per serving 23.1fat; 1602kJ (383 cal)
tip Dressing can be made up to three days ahead.

chicken tandoori pockets with raita

PREPARATION TIME **10 MINUTES**   COOKING TIME **10 MINUTES**

1 tablespoon lime juice
$^1/_3$ cup (100g) tandoori paste
$^1/_4$ cup (70g) yogurt
400g chicken tenderloins
8 large flour tortillas
60g snow pea tendrils

RAITA
1 cup (280g) yogurt
1 lebanese cucumber (130g), halved, seeded, chopped finely
1 tablespoon finely chopped fresh mint

1 Combine juice, paste and yogurt in medium bowl; add chicken, toss to coat chicken in marinade.
2 Cook chicken, in batches, on heated oiled grill plate (or grill or barbecue) until cooked through. Stand 5 minutes; slice thickly
3 Meanwhile, heat tortillas according to manufacturer's instructions.
4 Place equal amounts of the chicken, tendrils and raita on a quarter section of each tortilla; fold tortilla in half and then in half again to enclose filling and form triangle-shaped pockets.
raita Combine ingredients in small bowl.

makes 8
per pocket 8.8g fat; 1003kJ (240 cal)

chicken and bean salad

PREPARATION TIME 15 MINUTES   COOKING TIME 5 MINUTES

You need to purchase a large barbecued chicken weighing approximately 900g for this recipe.

350g yellow string beans, trimmed, halved
1 teaspoon finely grated lime rind
2 tablespoons lime juice
1 tablespoon grated palm sugar
1 clove garlic, crushed
1 tablespoon peanut oil
$^1/_2$ cup finely chopped fresh mint
2 teaspoons sweet chilli sauce
1 tablespoon fish sauce
2$^1/_2$ cups (400g) shredded cooked chicken
1 cup coarsely chopped fresh coriander
250g cherry tomatoes, halved
1 small fresh red thai chilli, chopped finely

1 Boil, steam or microwave beans until almost tender. Rinse under cold water; drain.
2 Meanwhile, combine rind, juice, sugar, garlic, oil, mint and sauces in large bowl.
3 Add beans, chicken, three quarters of the coriander and tomato; toss gently to combine.
4 Top salad with remaining coriander and chilli.

serves 4
per serving 13.6g fat; 1136kJ (272 cal)
tip Chopped snake beans can be substituted for yellow string beans.
serving suggestion Salad also can be served in lettuce or cabbage leaves.

chicken, witlof and cashew salad

PREPARATION TIME 20 MINUTES

Like mushrooms, witlof is grown in the dark to retain its pale colour and bittersweet taste. Sometimes spelled witloof, and also known as belgian endive or chicory, this versatile vegetable is as good eaten cooked as it is raw. You need to purchase a large barbecued chicken weighing approximately 900g for this recipe.

1 medium witlof (125g)

2 baby cos lettuces

1 medium yellow capsicum (200g),
   sliced thinly

1 small red onion (100g), sliced thinly

1 cup (150g) roasted unsalted cashews

2½ cups (400g) shredded
   cooked chicken

DRESSING

1 cup (280g) yogurt

2 cloves garlic, crushed

2 teaspoons finely grated lemon rind

¼ cup (60ml) lemon juice

¼ cup coarsely chopped
   fresh coriander

1 Trim and discard 1cm from witlof base; separate leaves. Trim core from lettuce; separate leaves.

2 Place witlof and lettuce in large bowl with capsicum, onion, cashews, chicken and dressing; toss gently to combine.

dressing Combine ingredients in screw-top jar; shake well.

serves 4

per serving 31g fat; 2167kJ (518 cal)

tips Roast cashews briefly in a small dry heavy-based frying pan, stirring, over medium heat, to bring out their flavour.

chicken and thai basil stir-fry

PREPARATION TIME 20 MINUTES COOKING TIME 15 MINUTES

2 tablespoons peanut oil
600g chicken breast fillets, sliced thinly
2 cloves garlic, crushed
1cm piece fresh ginger (5g), grated finely
4 small fresh red thai chillies, sliced thinly
4 kaffir lime leaves, shredded
1 medium brown onion (150g), sliced thinly
100g button mushrooms, quartered
1 large carrot (180g), sliced thinly
¼ cup (60ml) oyster sauce
1 tablespoon soy sauce
1 tablespoon fish sauce
$^1/_3$ cup (80ml) chicken stock
1 cup (80g) bean sprouts
¾ cup loosely packed fresh thai basil leaves

1 Heat half of the oil in wok or large frying pan; stir-fry chicken, in batches, until browned all over and cooked through.
2 Heat remaining oil in wok; stir-fry garlic, ginger, chilli, lime leaves and onion until onion softens and mixture is fragrant.
3 Add mushroom and carrot; stir-fry until carrot is just tender. Return chicken to wok with sauces and stock; stir-fry until sauce thickens slightly. Remove from heat; toss bean sprouts and basil leaves through stir-fry.

serves 4
per serving 18.2g fat; 1449kJ (346 cal)

sticky barbecue wings

PREPARATION TIME 10 MINUTES   COOKING TIME 25 MINUTES

12 chicken wings (1kg)
$^1/_4$ cup (60ml) barbecue sauce
$^1/_4$ cup (60ml) plum sauce
1 tablespoon worcestershire sauce

1 Preheat oven to hot.
2 Cut wing tips from chicken; cut wings in half at joint.
3 Combine sauces in large bowl. Add chicken; toss to coat chicken all over. Place chicken, in single layer, in large oiled baking dish; roast, uncovered, in hot oven about 25 minutes or until chicken is cooked through.

serves 4
per serving 8.5g fat; 1204kJ (288 cal)

peanut-crusted thai chicken

PREPARATION TIME 10 MINUTES   COOKING TIME 20 MINUTES

1 cup (150g) roasted unsalted peanuts
¼ cup (75g) red curry paste
1 tablespoon kecap manis
½ cup (125ml) coconut milk
1 cup coarsely chopped
**   fresh coriander**
500g chicken breast fillets
1 telegraph cucumber (400g)
2 cups bean sprouts (160g)
⅓ cup coarsely chopped fresh mint
1 medium red onion (170g), halved,
**   sliced thinly**
1 teaspoon fish sauce
2 tablespoons sweet chilli sauce
1 tablespoon lime juice
1 tablespoon peanut oil

1   Preheat oven to moderately hot.
2   Blend or process peanuts, paste, kecap manis, coconut milk and half of the coriander until just combined.
3   Place chicken, in single layer, on lightly oiled oven tray; spread peanut mixture on each piece. Roast, uncovered, in moderately hot oven about 20 minutes or until chicken is cooked through. Remove chicken from oven; stand 5 minutes, slice thickly.
4   Meanwhile, cut cucumber in half lengthways. Remove and discard seeds; slice thinly. Combine cucumber in large bowl with sprouts, mint, onion and remaining coriander.
5   Combine sauces, juice and oil in screw-top jar; shake well. Pour dressing over cucumber salad; toss gently to combine. Serve chicken with salad.

serves 4
per serving 40g fat; 2452kJ (585 cal)
tip The reason you rest chicken after removing it from the oven is to let the juices settle, making it easier to slice.

thai chicken in lettuce-leaf cups

PREPARATION TIME 20 MINUTES

*You need to purchase a large barbecued chicken
weighing approximately 900g for this recipe.*

8 large iceberg lettuce leaves
1 tablespoon kecap manis
1 tablespoon sesame oil
1 tablespoon lime juice
1 large zucchini (150g), grated coarsely
1 medium carrot (120g), grated coarsely
2 green onions, sliced thinly
1 medium red capsicum (200g), sliced thinly
2½ cups (400g) shredded cooked chicken
1 tablespoon finely chopped fresh mint
2 tablespoons coarsely chopped fresh coriander
2 tablespoons sweet chilli sauce

1 Trim lettuce-leaf edges with scissors. Place leaves in large bowl of iced water; refrigerate.
2 Meanwhile, combine kecap manis, oil and juice in large bowl. Add zucchini, carrot, onion, capsicum, chicken, mint and half of the coriander; toss gently to combine.
3 Dry lettuce; divide leaves among serving plates. Top with chicken mixture; drizzle with combined sweet chilli sauce and remaining coriander.

serves 4
per serving 13.7g fat; 1087kJ (260 cal)

char-grilled five-spice chicken

PREPARATION TIME 15 MINUTES COOKING TIME 10 MINUTES

750g chicken tenderloins
1 teaspoon peanut oil
1¹/₂ teaspoons five-spice powder
2 cloves garlic, crushed
300g baby corncobs
500g asparagus
1 medium red capsicum (200g),
  sliced thinly
¹/₄ cup coarsely chopped fresh
  flat-leaf parsley

1 Combine chicken, oil, five-spice and garlic in medium bowl.
2 Cook chicken on heated oiled grill plate (or grill or barbecue) until browned and cooked through.
3 Meanwhile, cut baby corncobs in half. Snap woody ends off asparagus; chop remaining spears into same-sized pieces as halved corn. Stir-fry corn, asparagus and capsicum in heated lightly oiled wok or large frying pan until just tender.
4 Stir parsley into vegetables off the heat, then divide mixture among serving bowls; top with sliced chicken.

serves 4
per serving 16.1g fat; 1646kJ (392 cal)

salt and pepper chicken skewers on baby bok choy

PREPARATION TIME 10 MINUTES COOKING TIME 15 MINUTES

**800g chicken thigh fillets,
   chopped coarsely**
**1 teaspoon sichuan
   peppercorns, crushed**
$1/2$ teaspoon five-spice powder
2 teaspoons sea salt
1 teaspoon sesame oil
600g baby bok choy, quartered
1 tablespoon oyster sauce
1 teaspoon light soy sauce
1 tablespoon chopped fresh coriander

1 Thread chicken onto 12 skewers. Combine peppercorns, five-spice and salt in small bowl; sprinkle mixture over chicken, pressing in firmly.
2 Cook chicken, in batches, on heated oiled grill plate (or grill or barbecue) until browned all over and cooked through; cover to keep warm.
3 Meanwhile, heat oil in wok or large frying pan; stir-fry bok choy with combined sauces until wilted.
4 Divide bok choy among serving plates; top with chicken skewers. Sprinkle chicken with coriander. Serve with steamed white rice, if desired.

serves 4
per serving 15.8g fat; 1289kJ (308 cal)

pesto chicken salad

PREPARATION TIME 5 MINUTES (PLUS STANDING TIME)
COOKING TIME 15 MINUTES

$^1/_3$ cup (90g) basil pesto
2 tablespoons balsamic vinegar
500g chicken breast fillets
6 medium egg tomatoes (450g), halved
125g baby rocket leaves
1 tablespoon olive oil

1 Combine pesto and vinegar in small bowl.
2 Place chicken and tomato on large tray; brush half of the
   pesto mixture over both.
3 Cook tomato on heated oiled grill plate (or grill or barbecue)
   until just softened; remove from plate. Cook chicken on same
   grill plate until browned both sides and cooked through. Stand
   5 minutes; slice thickly.
4 Place tomato and chicken in large bowl with rocket. Add oil
   and remaining pesto mixture; toss gently to combine.

serves 4
per serving 7.8g fat; 873kJ (209 cal)
tip You can substitute mixed lettuce leaves for the baby rocket.
serving suggestion Sprinkle with shaved parmesan cheese.

chicken and mixed mushroom stir-fry

PREPARATION TIME 15 MINUTES COOKING TIME 10 MINUTES

600g hokkien noodles
1 tablespoon peanut oil
750g chicken tenderloins, halved
200g button mushrooms, halved
200g flat mushrooms, sliced thickly
200g swiss brown mushrooms, halved
3 green onions, chopped finely
2 tablespoons mild chilli sauce
¹/₂ cup (125ml) oyster sauce

1 Rinse noodles in strainer under hot water. Separate noodles with fork; drain.
2 Heat half of the oil in wok or large frying pan; stir-fry chicken, in batches, until browned all over and cooked through.
3 Heat remaining oil in wok; stir-fry mushrooms, in batches, until browned. Return chicken and mushrooms to wok with noodles, onion and sauces; stir-fry until heated through.

serves 4
per serving 16.5g fat; 2342kJ (560 cal)
tip Also known as roman mushrooms, swiss browns have a strong, earthy flavour.

chicken with parsley and lemon

PREPARATION TIME 15 MINUTES   COOKING TIME 15 MINUTES

8 chicken thigh fillets (1kg)
¹/₃ cup (50g) plain flour
1 tablespoon olive oil
20g butter
1 cup coarsely chopped fresh
    flat-leaf parsley
2 tablespoons lemon juice

POLENTA
3 cups (750ml) hot water
1 cup (250ml) chicken stock
1 cup (170g) instant polenta
20g butter
¹/₂ cup (40g) grated parmesan cheese

1   Make polenta.
2   Meanwhile, toss chicken in flour; shake away excess flour. Heat oil and butter in large frying pan, add chicken and cook until browned both sides and cooked through. Add parsley and lemon juice, stir to coat chicken.
3   Serve chicken with polenta and steamed green beans, if desired.
    polenta Combine the water and stock in large saucepan, bring to a boil, reduce heat to a simmer. Gradually whisk in polenta and cook, uncovered, stirring frequently, about 5 minutes or until mixture is thick and soft. Stir in butter and parmesan.

serves 4
per serving 35.3g fat; 2923kJ (698 cal)

chicken with mustard and sun-dried tomato sauce

PREPARATION TIME 10 MINUTES COOKING TIME 15 MINUTES

30g butter
1 clove garlic, crushed
4 single chicken breast fillets (680g)
$^3/_4$ cup (180ml) chicken stock
1 tablespoon wholegrain mustard
$^1/_4$ cup (35g) drained sun-dried tomatoes, chopped finely
4 green onions, chopped finely

1 Heat butter in large frying pan; cook garlic, stirring, 1 minute. Add chicken to pan; cook on both sides until browned lightly and cooked through. Remove chicken from pan.
2 Add stock to pan; bring to a boil. Reduce heat; simmer, uncovered, 5 minutes. Stir in mustard and tomato. Stir in onion.
3 Serve sliced chicken with sauce.

serves 4
per serving 10.7g fat; 1155kJ (276 cal)

chicken and chinese broccoli stir-fry

PREPARATION TIME 10 MINUTES COOKING TIME 15 MINUTES

350g fresh singapore noodles
1 tablespoon peanut oil
750g chicken tenderloins, halved
1 large brown onion (200g),
    sliced thickly
3 cloves garlic, crushed
1kg chinese broccoli, chopped coarsely
¹/₃ cup (80ml) oyster sauce
1 tablespoon light soy sauce

1 Rinse noodles in strainer under hot water. Separate noodles with fork; drain.
2 Heat half of the oil in wok or large frying pan; stir-fry chicken, in batches, until browned all over and cooked through.
3 Heat remaining oil in wok; stir-fry onion and garlic until onion softens.
4 Return chicken to wok with broccoli and sauces; stir-fry until broccoli just wilts.
5 Toss chicken mixture with noodles to serve.

serves 4
per serving 32.9g fat; 3382kJ (809 cal)
tip Any type of fresh noodle can be used in this recipe.

garlic chicken stir-fry with bok choy

PREPARATION TIME 15 MINUTES   COOKING TIME 10 MINUTES

750g chicken breast fillets,
**   sliced thinly**
$1/2$ cup (75g) plain flour
2 tablespoons peanut oil
6 cloves garlic, crushed
1 medium red capsicum (200g),
**   sliced thinly**
6 green onions, sliced thinly
$1/2$ cup (125ml) chicken stock
2 tablespoons light soy sauce
500g bok choy, chopped coarsely

1   Coat chicken in flour; shake off excess flour.
2   Heat oil in wok or large frying pan; stir-fry chicken, in batches, until browned all over and cooked through.
3   Add garlic, capsicum and onion to wok; stir-fry until capsicum is tender.
4   Return chicken to wok with stock and sauce; stir-fry until sauce boils and thickens slightly. Add bok choy; stir-fry until bok choy just wilts.

serves 4
per serving 20.4g fat; 1838kJ (440 cal)
tip You can substitute any asian green for the bok choy.
serving suggestion This dish goes nicely with crispy fried noodles or steamed white rice.

satay drumettes

PREPARATION TIME 5 MINUTES COOKING TIME 25 MINUTES

Drumettes are, in fact, wings trimmed to resemble drumsticks; in some areas, this name is used (along with lovely legs) when describing pared-back and trimmed drumsticks. You can use either in this recipe.

1kg chicken drumettes
¹/₄ cup (60ml) kecap manis
2 cups (400g) jasmine rice
³/₄ cup (210g) crunchy peanut butter
²/₃ cup (160ml) chicken stock
2 tablespoons sweet chilli sauce
1 tablespoon light soy sauce
1 tablespoon lemon juice
1 cup (250ml) coconut milk

1 Preheat oven to hot.
2 Place chicken, in single layer, in large shallow oiled baking dish; brush chicken all over with kecap manis. Roast, uncovered, in hot oven about 25 minutes or until chicken is cooked through.
3 Meanwhile, cook rice in large saucepan of boiling water, uncovered, until just tender; drain. Cover to keep warm.
4 Combine peanut butter, stock, sauces, juice and coconut milk in medium saucepan; bring to a boil. Reduce heat; simmer, uncovered, 5 minutes.
5 Serve rice and chicken drizzled with satay sauce.

serves 4
per serving 47.1g fat; 4157kJ (993 cal)
tip You can also cook the drumettes on a grill or barbecue.

thai green curry

PREPARATION TIME 10 MINUTES COOKING TIME 15 MINUTES

1 large brown onion (200g),
chopped coarsely
2 cloves garlic, crushed
4cm piece fresh ginger (20g),
grated finely
1 tablespoon finely sliced
fresh lemon grass
2 tablespoons green curry paste
500g chicken breast fillets,
sliced thickly
1 tablespoon peanut oil
³/₄ cup (180ml) chicken stock
1²/₃ cups (400ml) coconut milk
2 tablespoons lime juice
230g can sliced bamboo shoots, drained
300g fresh baby corn, halved
¹/₂ cup coarsely chopped
fresh coriander

1 Combine onion, garlic, ginger, lemon grass and paste in medium bowl. Add chicken; toss to coat in mixture. Heat oil in wok or large frying pan; stir-fry chicken mixture, in batches, until chicken is just browned.

2 Return chicken mixture to wok with stock, coconut milk and juice; cook, uncovered, about 5 minutes or until curry mixture thickens slightly and chicken is cooked through.

3 Reduce heat. Add bamboo shoots, corn and coriander; stir-fry until heated through.

serves 4
per serving 37g fat; 2315kJ (554 cal)
serving suggestion Serve this curry with steamed long-grain white rice.

butter chicken

PREPARATION TIME 5 MINUTES COOKING TIME 25 MINUTES

In India, chicken is regarded as a delicacy, and the mouth-watering flavour of butter chicken, also known as murgh makhani, is a real treat. This famous dish, featuring chicken simmered in a rich, creamy tomato and butter sauce, is a delicious addition to any Indian banquet.

80g butter

1 medium brown onion (150g),
   chopped finely

3 cloves garlic, crushed

3 teaspoons sweet paprika

2 teaspoons garam masala

2 teaspoons ground coriander

1/2 teaspoon chilli powder

1 cinnamon stick

2 tablespoons white vinegar

425g can tomato puree

3/4 cup (180ml) chicken stock

1 tablespoon tomato paste

750g chicken thigh fillets, quartered

1 cup (250ml) cream

1/2 cup (140g) yogurt

1 Melt butter in large saucepan; cook onion, garlic and spices, stirring, until onion softens.

2 Add vinegar, puree, stock and paste; bring to a boil. Reduce heat; simmer, uncovered, 10 minutes, stirring occasionally.

3 Add chicken to pan with cream and yogurt; bring to a boil. Reduce heat; simmer, uncovered, about 10 minutes or until chicken is cooked through. Remove and discard cinnamon stick before serving.

serves 4

per serving 59.2g fat; 3124kJ (747 cal)

tip In India, this dish is often made using leftover tandoori chicken pieces; it can also be made using chicken breast fillets, if you prefer.

serving suggestion Serve butter chicken with cucumber raita, boiled or steamed basmati rice and warm naan bread.

chicken, pide and haloumi salad

PREPARATION TIME **10 MINUTES** COOKING TIME **15 MINUTES**

300g prepared mixed vegetable antipasto
500g chicken tenderloins, chopped coarsely
2 tablespoons pine nuts
¹/₂ long loaf pide
250g haloumi cheese
200g baby rocket leaves
170g marinated artichoke hearts, drained, quartered
250g cherry tomatoes
¹/₄ cup (60ml) balsamic vinegar

1 Drain antipasto in strainer over small bowl; reserve ⅓ cup of the oil. Chop antipasto finely.

2 Heat 1 tablespoon of the reserved oil in wok or large frying pan; stir-fry chicken, in batches, until browned all over and cooked through. Cover to keep warm. Stir-fry pine nuts in same wok until lightly browned.

3 Cut pide into 1cm slices; grill until browned both sides. Cut haloumi crossways into 16 slices. Heat 1 tablespoon of the reserved oil in same wok; cook haloumi, in batches, until browned both sides.

4 Toss antipasto, chicken, pide and haloumi in large bowl with rocket, artichoke and tomatoes. Drizzle with combined remaining oil and vinegar; sprinkle with pine nuts.

serves 4
per serving 47.8g fat; 3335kJ (798 cal)
tips Haloumi is a firm salty cheese, available from most delicatessens and some supermarkets.
If there is not enough oil in the mixed vegetable antipasto to make ⅓ cup, add olive oil to make up the required amount.

oven-baked parmesan chicken

PREPARATION TIME 15 MINUTES COOKING TIME 15 MINUTES

Curly endive, also known as frisée, is a loose-headed green vegetable having curly, ragged edged leaves and a slightly bitter flavour. It is usually used as a salad green, but in Europe it is also eaten as a cooked vegetable and in making soups.

1 tablespoon plain flour
2 eggs, beaten lightly
2 cups (140g) stale breadcrumbs
$^1/_3$ cup (25g) coarsely grated
    parmesan cheese
2 tablespoons finely chopped
    fresh flat-leaf parsley
12 chicken tenderloins (900g)
1 cup firmly packed fresh basil leaves
$^1/_2$ cup (125ml) olive oil
$^1/_4$ cup (60ml) lemon juice
1 clove garlic, quartered
$^3/_4$ cup (120g) kalamata olives, seeded
200g curly endive
40g baby rocket leaves

1 Preheat oven to hot.
2 Combine flour and egg in medium bowl; combine breadcrumbs, cheese and parsley in another medium bowl. Coat chicken, one piece at a time, first in flour mixture then in breadcrumb mixture. Place chicken, in single layer, on oiled oven tray; roast, uncovered, in hot oven about 15 minutes or until chicken is lightly browned and cooked through.
3 Meanwhile, blend or process basil, oil, juice and garlic until dressing is well combined.
4 Serve chicken with combined olives, endive and rocket; drizzle with basil dressing.

serves 4
per serving 47.3g fat; 3320kJ (794 cal)

coriander and chilli grilled fillets

PREPARATION TIME 10 MINUTES   COOKING TIME 15 MINUTES

700g chicken thigh fillets, halved

CORIANDER CHILLI SAUCE
8 green onions, chopped coarsely
3 cloves garlic, quartered
3 small fresh red thai chillies,
**   seeded, chopped coarsely**
¼ cup loosely packed fresh
**   coriander leaves**
1 teaspoon sugar
1 tablespoon fish sauce
¼ cup (60ml) lime juice

CHICKPEA SALAD
2 x 300g cans chickpeas, rinsed, drained
2 medium egg tomatoes (150g),
**   chopped coarsely**
2 green onions, chopped finely
2 tablespoons lime juice
1 cup coarsely chopped fresh coriander
1 tablespoon olive oil

1   Cook chicken, in batches, on heated oiled grill plate (or grill or barbecue) until almost cooked through. Brush about two-thirds of the coriander chilli sauce all over chicken; cook further 5 minutes or until chicken is cooked through.

2   Serve chicken, sprinkled with remaining coriander chilli sauce, with chickpea salad.

coriander chilli sauce Blend or process onion, garlic, chilli, coriander and sugar until finely chopped. Add fish sauce and juice; blend until well combined.

chickpea salad Combine ingredients in large bowl; toss to combine.

serves 4
per serving 19.3g fat; 1665kJ (398 cal)

chicken in red wine and tomato sauce

PREPARATION TIME 10 MINUTES COOKING TIME 20 MINUTES

30g butter
2 tablespoons olive oil
2 medium white onions (300g), sliced thinly
2 cloves garlic, crushed
750g chicken thigh fillets, halved
250g button mushrooms, sliced thinly
2 x 410g cans tomatoes
$^1/_4$ cup (60ml) tomato paste
$^1/_4$ cup (60ml) dry red wine
2 teaspoons brown sugar
1 teaspoon cracked black peppercorns
$^1/_2$ cup (125ml) chicken stock
$^1/_4$ cup finely chopped fresh basil

1 Heat butter and oil in large saucepan; cook onion and garlic, stirring, until onion is soft. Add chicken; cook until cooked through.
2 Stir in mushroom, undrained crushed tomatoes, paste, wine, sugar, peppercorns and stock.
3 Bring to a boil; reduce heat. Simmer, uncovered, until sauce has thickened slightly. Remove from heat; stir in basil.

serves 4
per serving 29.6g fat; 2086kJ (498 cal)
tip Recipe can be made a day ahead and refrigerated, covered.

chicken chermoulla

PREPARATION TIME 10 MINUTES COOKING TIME 20 MINUTES

Chermoulla is a Moroccan blend of herbs and spices traditionally used for preserving or seasoning meat and fish. We use our chermoulla blend here as a quick baste for chicken, but you can also make it for use as a sauce or marinade.

700g chicken thigh fillets, sliced thinly
$1/2$ cup coarsely chopped fresh
   flat-leaf parsley
1 tablespoon finely grated lemon rind
1 tablespoon lemon juice
2 teaspoons ground turmeric
1 teaspoon cayenne pepper
1 tablespoon ground coriander
1 medium red onion (170g),
   chopped finely
2 tablespoons olive oil
1 cup (200g) red lentils
$2^1/2$ cups (625ml) chicken stock
200g baby spinach leaves
$1/2$ cup coarsely chopped
   fresh coriander
$1/2$ cup coarsely chopped fresh mint
1 tablespoon red wine vinegar
$1/3$ cup (95g) yogurt

1 Combine chicken, parsley, rind, juice, spices, onion and half of the oil in large bowl. Heat wok or large frying pan; stir-fry chicken mixture, in batches, until chicken is browned and cooked through.

2 Meanwhile, combine lentils and stock in large saucepan. Bring to a boil; reduce heat. Simmer, uncovered, about 8 minutes or until just tender; drain. Place lentils in large bowl with spinach, coriander, mint and combined vinegar and remaining oil; toss gently to combine.

3 Serve chicken mixture on lentil mixture; drizzle with yogurt.

serves 4
per serving 24.9g fat; 2191kJ (524 cal)

chicken salsa wraps

PREPARATION TIME 10 MINUTES COOKING TIME 10 MINUTES

800g chicken thigh fillets
2 teaspoons mexican seasoning
280g packet enchilada (corn) tortillas
2 large tomatoes (500g)
1 medium yellow capsicum (200g)
1 medium avocado (250g)
1 small red onion (100g)
1 tablespoon lime juice
1 tablespoon chopped fresh coriander

1 Sprinkle chicken with seasoning and cook, covered, on a heated oiled char-grill pan (or grill or barbecue) until browned on both sides and just cooked through. Slice chicken thinly.

2 Meanwhile, heat tortillas according to packet directions. Remove seeds from tomatoes. Chop tomatoes, capsicum, avocado and onion finely; transfer to medium bowl. Add juice and coriander.

3 Serve chicken and salsa wrapped in tortillas.

serves 4
per serving 28.2g fat; 2294kJ (548 cal)

Italian-style toasted sandwich

Cut a long loaf of pide in half horizontally, spread base with basil pesto, top with well drained char-grilled vegetables, basil leaves and cheddar cheese. Top with remaining bread; cut loaf into four squares, place in toasted-sandwich press until cheese melts.

potato and rosemary pizza

Sprinkle prepared pizza base with grated parmesan cheese, top with thinly sliced new potatoes, chopped fresh rosemary and thinly sliced garlic; lightly drizzle with olive oil. Bake in hot oven until top is lightly browned and base crisp.

goats cheese and garlic bruschetta

Cut a loaf of ciabatta into 1cm slices; brush one side of each slice with combined olive oil and crushed garlic. Grill bread until lightly browned on both sides. Spread oiled side of each slice with goats cheese, top with sliced red onion, rocket and black pepper; serve drizzled with olive oil.

tomato, zucchini and cheese tarts

Cut a sheet of ready-rolled puff pastry into quarters. Place pastry squares on lightly greased oven tray. Fold in pastry edges to make a 1cm border. Sprinkle a little grated parmesan cheese over pastry, top with halved cherry tomatoes and sliced baby zucchini, sprinkle with a little more parmesan cheese. Bake in very hot oven about 12 minutes or until pastry is puffed and browned.

chilli parmesan crisps

Combine finely grated parmesan cheese, chilli powder and finely chopped fresh coriander. Place tablespoons of mixture onto lightly oiled oven trays. Bake in moderately hot oven 5 minutes or until browned lightly. Stand 2 minutes; cool crisps on wire rack.

chilli popcorn

Cook popping corn with a little oil in large saucepan, covered, until corn stops popping; transfer mixture to bowl. Melt butter in small saucepan, add cayenne pepper, paprika and salt. Pour butter mixture over popcorn and toss well to combine.

sumac wedges

Cut potatoes in wedges, combine in large microwave-safe bowl with sumac and olive oil. Cook, covered, in microwave oven on HIGH (100%) until just cooked. Place wedges, in single layer, on lightly greased oven tray. Bake in very hot oven 20 minutes or until crisp. Sprinkle with sea salt.

chicken rice paper rolls

Combine shredded cooked chicken, grated carrot, sliced capsicum, snow pea tendrils, chopped fresh coriander and sweet chilli sauce. Place a rice paper round in medium bowl of warm water until just softened; lift sheet carefully onto board. Place some of the chicken mixture in centre of sheet; fold in sides, roll to enclose filling. Repeat with remaining rice paper and chicken mixture.

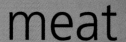
meat

From steaks and stir-fries to salads and wraps, meat is
one of the most versatile ingredients around. With such a
selection of beef, veal, lamb and pork available, there is no
end to the variety of dishes you can create. Fast-cooking
cuts limit the amount of time you spend in the kitchen.

hoisin beef stir-fry
with cabbage

PREPARATION TIME 20 MINUTES   COOKING TIME 15 MINUTES

¼ cup (60ml) peanut oil
4 cups (280g) coarsely shredded chinese cabbage
½ cup coarsely chopped fresh garlic chives
750g beef rump steak, sliced thinly
1 large red onion (300g), sliced thickly
2 cloves garlic, crushed
1cm piece fresh ginger (5g), grated finely
1 teaspoon five-spice powder
250g shiitake mushrooms, sliced thickly
1 large red capsicum (350g), sliced thinly
½ cup (125ml) hoisin sauce
1 tablespoon soy sauce
1 tablespoon rice wine vinegar

1 Heat 1 tablespoon of the oil in wok or large frying pan; stir-fry cabbage and chives until cabbage is wilted. Transfer to serving bowl; cover to keep warm.
2 Heat another 1 tablespoon oil in wok; stir-fry beef, in batches, until well browned.
3 Heat remaining oil in wok; stir-fry onion until soft. Add garlic, ginger, five-spice, mushroom and capsicum; stir-fry until vegetables are tender.
4 Return beef to wok. Add combined sauces and vinegar; cook, stirring, until heated through. Serve beef stir-fry on top of cabbage.

serves 4
per serving 24.7g fat; 2078kJ (496 cal)

satay beef and stir-fried vegetables

PREPARATION TIME 20 MINUTES   COOKING TIME 20 MINUTES

1 teaspoon peanut oil
500g lean beef topside, sliced thinly
1 large brown onion (200g), sliced thinly
1 clove garlic, crushed
2cm piece fresh ginger (10g), grated finely
2 small fresh red thai chillies, seeded,
   chopped finely
1 medium red capsicum (200g),
   chopped coarsely
1 medium green capsicum (200g),
   chopped coarsely
100g button mushrooms, halved
225g can bamboo shoots, drained
1 teaspoon curry powder
2 teaspoons cornflour
½ cup (125ml) chicken stock
¼ cup (70g) smooth peanut butter
2 tablespoons oyster sauce
1 tablespoon unsalted, roasted,
   coarsely chopped peanuts

1 Heat oil in wok or large frying pan; stir-fry beef, in batches, until browned all over.

2 Reheat wok; stir-fry onion and garlic until onion softens. Add ginger, chilli, capsicums, mushroom, bamboo shoots and curry powder; stir-fry until vegetables are just tender.

3 Blend cornflour with stock in small jug; pour into wok, stir to combine with vegetable mixture. Return beef to wok with peanut butter and oyster sauce; bring to a boil, stirring, until sauce boils and thickens slightly, and beef is cooked as desired. Stir in peanuts.

serves 4
per serving 15.8g fat; 1384kJ (331 cal)
tip You can use sliced lamb fillets or sliced chicken thigh fillets instead of the beef, if you prefer.

veal with capers and parsley

PREPARATION TIME 5 MINUTES   COOKING TIME 15 MINUTES

2 tablespoons olive oil
8 veal steaks (800g)
2 cloves garlic, crushed
1/2 cup (125ml) dry white wine
1/2 cup (125ml) beef stock
2 tablespoons chopped fresh
**   flat-leaf parsley**
1/4 cup (50g) coarsely chopped capers

1 Heat oil in large frying pan; cook veal over high heat, in batches, until browned both sides and cooked as desired. Remove from pan; cover to keep warm. Add garlic to pan; stir until fragrant.

2 Add wine to pan; bring to a boil. Add stock; reduce heat. Simmer, uncovered, 2 minutes; stir in parsley and capers. Slice veal.

3 Serve veal with sauce; accompany with mashed potato, if desired.

serves 4
per serving   14.3g fat; 1374kJ (328 cal)
tips Recipe best made just before serving. Capers are packed in brine or salt; rinse quickly before using.

steaks with corn and red capsicum salsa

PREPARATION TIME **15 MINUTES** COOKING TIME **15 MINUTES**

12 tiny new potatoes (480g), halved
4 beef rump steaks (1kg)

CORN AND RED CAPSICUM SALSA
1 large red capsicum (350g), chopped finely
1 small red onion (100g), chopped finely
1 small fresh red thai chilli, seeded, chopped finely
6 green onions, sliced thinly
¼ cup (60ml) lime juice
2 tablespoons finely chopped fresh mint
125g can corn kernels

1 Boil, steam or microwave potato until tender; drain.
2 Meanwhile, make corn and red capsicum salsa.
3 Cook beef on heated oiled grill plate (or grill or barbecue) until browned both sides and cooked as desired; serve with salsa and potato.
corn and red capsicum salsa Combine ingredients in medium bowl.

serves 4
per serving 13.4g fat; 1945kJ (465 cal)
tips The salsa can be made several hours ahead and refrigerated, covered.
Sirloin, scotch fillet or eye fillet can be substituted for the rump steaks.

thai beef salad

PREPARATION TIME 15 MINUTES (PLUS STANDING TIME) COOKING TIME 15 MINUTES

This dish, known in Thailand as yum nua, often has the major ingredients arranged separately on a platter; here, we've tossed them all together.

500g beef fillet

3 medium green cucumbers (510g),
   peeled, sliced thickly

4 small fresh red thai chillies, sliced thinly

3 green onions, sliced thinly

1/2 cup loosely packed fresh mint leaves

1/2 cup loosely packed fresh
   coriander leaves

LEMON GRASS DRESSING

1 clove garlic, crushed

2 teaspoons finely chopped lemon grass

2 teaspoons finely chopped fresh
   coriander root

1 tablespoon lime juice

2 tablespoons light soy sauce

1/2 teaspoon fish sauce

2 teaspoons brown sugar

1 Cook beef on heated oiled grill plate (or grill or barbecue) until browned all over and cooked as desired. Stand 5 minutes; slice thinly.

2 Place beef, cucumber, chilli, onion, herbs and lemon grass dressing in large bowl; toss gently to combine.
   lemon grass dressing Combine ingredients in small bowl.

serves 4
per serving 6.3g fat; 792kJ (189 cal)
tip If you're running short on time, you can substitute thin slices of rare roast beef for the beef fillet.
serving suggestion Serve with deep-fried crispy rice noodles, also known as mee krob or mee grob, for an authentic Thai experience.

teriyaki beef

PREPARATION TIME **10 MINUTES (PLUS STANDING TIME)** COOKING TIME **20 MINUTES**

One of the most popular Japanese grilled meat dishes, teriyaki is so easy to prepare at home. Here, we accompany it with fresh baby corn, but try it with grilled red capsicum strips or trimmed sugar snap peas, if you prefer.

¹/₂ cup (125ml) mirin
¹/₃ cup (80ml) light soy sauce
¹/₄ cup (55g) firmly packed brown sugar
1 tablespoon sake
4cm piece fresh ginger (20g),
**   grated finely**
1 clove garlic, crushed
1 teaspoon sesame oil
1 tablespoon sesame seeds
750g beef fillet, sliced thinly
300g fresh baby corn, halved
2 green onions, sliced thinly

1 Combine mirin, sauce, sugar, sake, ginger, garlic, oil and seeds in large bowl. Stir in beef and corn; stand 5 minutes.
2 Drain beef mixture over medium saucepan; reserve marinade.
3 Cook beef and corn, in batches, on heated oiled grill plate (or grill or barbecue) until browned all over and cooked as desired.
4 Meanwhile, bring marinade to a boil. Reduce heat; simmer, uncovered, 5 minutes.
5 Serve beef and corn drizzled with hot marinade; sprinkle with onion.

serves 4
per serving 12.7g fat; 1819kJ (435 cal)
tip You can substitute pork, fish or chicken for the beef, if you prefer.
serving suggestion Serve with boiled or stir-fried noodles.

veal with anchovy butter and polenta

PREPARATION TIME 10 MINUTES COOKING TIME 20 MINUTES

90g butter, softened
4 anchovy fillets, drained, chopped finely
2 teaspoons lemon juice
1 tablespoon coarsely chopped fresh dill
1$^{1}/_{2}$ cups (375ml) chicken stock
2 cups (500ml) milk
1 cup (170g) polenta
$^{1}/_{3}$ cup (25g) coarsely grated parmesan cheese
8 veal cutlets (1.2kg)
200g green beans, trimmed
200g yellow string beans, trimmed

1 Combine butter, anchovy, juice and dill in small bowl.
2 Bring stock and milk to the boil in large saucepan. Stir in polenta gradually; cook, stirring, until mixture thickens. Add cheese; stir until cheese melts.
3 Meanwhile, cook veal, in batches, on heated oiled grill plate (or grill or barbecue) until browned both sides and cooked as desired.
4 Boil, steam or microwave beans until just tender; drain.
5 Serve veal with polenta and beans; top with anchovy butter.

serves 4
per serving 31.8g fat; 2773kJ (663 cal)
tip Chicken, fish, beef, lamb and pork are all suitable substitutes for the veal.

warm chilli beef salad

PREPARATION TIME **15 MINUTES**   COOKING TIME **15 MINUTES**

The salad ingredients in this Thai specialty are cooked just long enough to warm them through. You will need half a medium chinese cabbage to make this recipe.

2 tablespoons peanut oil
750g beef fillets, sliced thinly
1 medium white onion (150g), sliced thinly
2 small fresh red thai chillies, seeded,
**   chopped finely**
3 cloves garlic, crushed
2 tablespoons light soy sauce
1 teaspoon fish sauce
1 tablespoon sweet chilli sauce
2 tablespoons lime juice
250g cherry tomatoes, halved
3 cups (210g) finely shredded
**   chinese cabbage**
³/₄ cup loosely packed fresh mint leaves
1 medium green cucumber (170g),
**   seeded, sliced thinly**
1 cup (80g) bean sprouts

1   Heat half of the oil in wok or large frying pan; stir-fry beef, in batches, until browned all over.
2   Heat remaining oil in wok; stir-fry onion, chilli and garlic until onion softens.
3   Return beef to wok with combined sauces, juice, tomato and cabbage; stir-fry until cabbage just wilts.
4   Place beef mixture in large serving bowl. Stir in mint, cucumber and sprouts; serve immediately.

serves 4
per serving   18.7g fat; 1554kJ (372 cal)
tip   Place beef in freezer, in plastic wrap, for about 1 hour before use to make it easier to slice.
serving suggestion   Serve with a bowl of sambal oelek, the fiery-hot Indonesian chilli and vinegar condiment.

beef donburi

PREPARATION TIME **15 MINUTES** COOKING TIME **10 MINUTES**

*Donburi refers to a certain size of rice bowl, usually with a lid, and also the meat or poultry/rice combination
that is served in it. Koshihikari rice is grown from Japanese seed; substitute medium-grain white rice if desired.*

1 cup (200g) koshihikari rice
500g beef rump steak, sliced thinly
1 clove garlic, crushed
**1cm piece fresh ginger (5g),
    grated finely**
¹/₂ cup (125ml) light soy sauce
¹/₂ cup (125ml) mirin
1 tablespoon peanut oil
6 green onions, sliced thinly

1 Cook rice in large saucepan of boiling water, uncovered, until just tender; drain.
2 Meanwhile, combine beef, garlic and ginger in medium bowl with half of the soy
   sauce and half of the mirin.
3 Heat oil in large frying pan; cook beef, in batches, stirring, until browned all over.
   Return beef to pan with remaining soy sauce and mirin; bring to a boil.
4 Serve beef mixture over rice in bowls; sprinkle with onion.

serves 4
per serving 10.6g fat; 1794kJ (429 cal)
tip You can use thinly sliced chicken breast fillets rather than beef in this
recipe; if you do, thinly slice a large brown onion and add it to the chicken
mixture before cooking.

steaks with olives and sun-dried tomatoes

PREPARATION TIME 15 MINUTES COOKING TIME 20 MINUTES

1 teaspoon cracked black pepper
4 beef rib-eye steaks (800g)
1 tablespoon olive oil
1 medium red onion (170g), sliced thinly
3 cloves garlic, crushed
$^1/_3$ cup (80ml) brandy
410g can tomatoes
$^1/_2$ cup (75g) sun-dried tomatoes, drained, sliced thinly
$^1/_3$ cup (40g) seeded black olives, sliced thinly
1 teaspoon caster sugar
2 tablespoons small fresh basil leaves

1 Rub pepper onto both sides of each steak; heat oil in large frying pan. Cook steaks until browned both sides and cooked as desired; remove steaks from pan.

2 Add onion and garlic to pan; cook, stirring, until onion is soft. Add brandy to pan.

3 Stir in undrained crushed tomatoes, sun-dried tomatoes, olives and sugar; bring to a boil. Reduce heat; simmer, uncovered, 2 minutes. Serve sauce over steaks; sprinkle with basil. Accompany with fried potato slices and green salad, if desired.

serves 4
per serving 18.2g fat; 1882kJ (450 cal)
tip Recipe best made just before serving.

peanut beef curry

PREPARATION TIME 20 MINUTES   COOKING TIME 15 MINUTES

This hot and spicy curry combines the best of two countries – the fragrant spices of Indian cooking and the coconut-and-citrus flavours of the Thai kitchen. While we've chosen snow peas as the vegetable component, you can use any vegetable you have on hand – even potatoes.

1 tablespoon vegetable oil
750g beef fillet, sliced thinly
1¼ cups (310ml) coconut milk
½ cup (75g) roasted peanuts
1 tablespoon brown sugar
1 tablespoon cornflour
⅓ cup (80ml) lime juice
250g snow peas

CURRY PASTE
2 tablespoons vegetable oil
5 cloves garlic, crushed
4cm piece fresh ginger (20g), grated finely
4 green onions, chopped coarsely
1 tablespoon coarsely chopped lemon grass
1 tablespoon dried chilli flakes
1 teaspoon ground cumin
1 tablespoon ground coriander
1 teaspoon shrimp paste
1 cup (250ml) coconut milk

1 Heat oil in wok or large frying pan; stir-fry beef, in batches, until browned all over.

2 Return beef to wok with coconut milk, peanuts, sugar and curry paste; bring to a boil. Reduce heat; simmer, uncovered, about 10 minutes or until beef is tender.

3 Add blended cornflour and juice; bring to a boil. Reduce heat; simmer, uncovered, until sauce thickens.

4 Add snow peas; toss gently to combine.

curry paste Heat oil in medium saucepan; cook garlic, ginger, onion, lemon grass, spices and paste, stirring, until fragrant. Blend or process garlic mixture with coconut milk until smooth.

serves 4
per serving 60.5g fat; 3367kJ (804 cal)
tip Preparing a large quantity of curry paste in a food processor makes blending much easier and smoother; however, if you intend to keep the paste for future use, leave out the coconut milk. Place curry paste in a jar, seal it tightly, and refrigerate for up to four months.
serving suggestion The ideal accompaniment to this curry is a large platter of steamed or boiled jasmine rice and a bowl of minted yogurt.

veal with mushrooms and mustard cream sauce

PREPARATION TIME 5 MINUTES   COOKING TIME 20 MINUTES

1 tablespoon olive oil

8 veal steaks (800g)

10g butter

1 clove garlic, crushed

150g button mushrooms, sliced thickly

$\frac{1}{3}$ cup (80ml) dry white wine

1 tablespoon wholegrain mustard

$\frac{1}{2}$ cup (125ml) cream

$\frac{1}{4}$ cup (60ml) chicken stock

1 teaspoon fresh thyme leaves

1 Heat oil in large frying pan; cook veal, in batches, until browned both sides and cooked as desired. Cover to keep warm.

2 Melt butter in same pan; cook garlic and mushroom, stirring, until mushroom is just soft. Add wine and mustard; cook, stirring, 2 minutes. Add cream and stock; bring to a boil. Reduce heat; simmer, uncovered, about 5 minutes or until sauce thickens slightly. Stir in thyme.

3 Divide veal equally among serving plates; top with sauce. Serve veal with farfalle (bow-tie pasta), if desired.

serves 4

per serving 24.4g fat; 1612kJ (385 cal)

ginger beef stir-fry

PREPARATION TIME 20 MINUTES COOKING TIME 10 MINUTES

30g piece fresh ginger
2 tablespoons peanut oil
600g beef rump steak, sliced thinly
2 cloves garlic, crushed
120g snake beans, cut into 5cm lengths
8 green onions, sliced thinly
2 teaspoons grated palm sugar
2 teaspoons oyster sauce
1 tablespoon fish sauce
1 tablespoon soy sauce
½ cup loosely packed fresh thai basil leaves

1 Slice peeled ginger thinly; stack slices, then slice again into thin slivers.
2 Heat half of the oil in wok; stir-fry beef, in batches, until browned all over.
3 Heat remaining oil in wok; stir-fry ginger and garlic until fragrant. Add beans; stir-fry until just tender.
4 Return beef to wok with onion, sugar and sauces; stir-fry until sugar dissolves and beef is cooked as desired. Remove from heat, toss basil leaves through stir-fry.

serves 4
per serving 19.8g fat; 1536kJ (367 cal)

red beef curry

PREPARATION TIME 10 MINUTES   COOKING TIME 20 MINUTES

2 tablespoons peanut oil
500g beef rump, cut into 2cm pieces
1 large brown onion (200g), sliced thinly
¼ cup (75g) red curry paste
1 large red capsicum (350g), sliced thinly
150g snake beans, chopped
1²/₃ cups (400ml) coconut milk
425g can crushed tomatoes
¼ cup coarsely chopped fresh coriander

1   Heat half of the oil in wok or large frying pan; stir-fry beef, in batches, until browned all over.

2   Heat remaining oil in wok; stir-fry onion until soft. Add paste; stir-fry until fragrant. Add capsicum and snake beans; stir-fry until vegetables just soften.

3   Return beef to wok with remaining ingredients; stir-fry until sauce thickens slightly.

serves 4
per serving 41.9g fat; 2390kJ (571 cal)

char-grilled veal with tomato, capers and basil

PREPARATION TIME 15 MINUTES   COOKING TIME 15 MINUTES

6 baby eggplant (360g),
   halved lengthways
6 small zucchini (540g),
   halved lengthways
1/3 cup (80ml) extra virgin olive oil
12 veal cutlets (1.8kg)
2 medium egg tomatoes (230g),
   seeded, chopped finely
1/2 small red onion (50g),
   chopped finely
1 clove garlic, crushed
2 tablespoons small capers,
   rinsed, drained
1 tablespoon balsamic vinegar
1 tablespoon baby basil leaves

1 Brush eggplant and zucchini with half the oil; cook, in batches, on heated grill plate (or grill or barbecue) until browned and tender. Transfer to a plate; cover to keep warm.

2 Cook veal on heated oiled grill plate until browned on both sides and cooked as desired. Transfer to a plate and cover; stand 10 minutes.

3 Meanwhile, combine tomato, onion, garlic, capers, vinegar and remaining oil in a small bowl.

4 Divide eggplant and zucchini among serving plates, top with cutlets and tomato mixture. Sprinkle with basil leaves.

serves 6
per serving 18.1g fat; 1683kJ (402 cal)
tip Antipasto eggplant and zucchini may be used instead of fresh for a quicker alternative.

lamb cutlets with sweet citrus sauce

PREPARATION TIME **10 MINUTES** COOKING TIME **20 MINUTES**

2 tablespoons olive oil
8 lamb cutlets (600g)

SWEET CITRUS SAUCE
1 tablespoon grated orange rind
$^1/_3$ cup (80ml) orange juice
2 tablespoons lemon juice
$^1/_2$ cup (125ml) redcurrant jelly
1 tablespoon red wine vinegar

1 Heat oil in large frying pan; cook lamb until tender.
2 Serve lamb with sweet citrus sauce; accompany with mashed potatoes and rocket, if desired.
sweet citrus sauce Combine rind, juices, jelly and vinegar in medium saucepan; stir over heat until jelly melts. Bring to a boil; reduce heat. Simmer, uncovered, until sauce boils and thickens slightly.

serves 4
per serving 21.9g fat; 1559kJ (373 cal)
tip Sauce can be made a day ahead and refrigerated, covered.

warm lamb salad with sun-dried tomatoes

PREPARATION TIME 20 MINUTES   COOKING TIME 15 MINUTES

500g lamb fillets
1 clove garlic, crushed
¹/₄ cup (60ml) balsamic vinegar
¹/₃ cup (80ml) olive oil
¹/₃ cup (50g) drained sun-dried
   tomatoes, sliced thickly
15g butter
250g fresh asparagus, chopped coarsely
1 medium red capsicum (200g),
   chopped coarsely
150g button mushrooms, quartered
80g baby rocket leaves

1 Cook lamb in heated large non-stick frying pan until browned and cooked as desired; slice lamb. Combine lamb, garlic, vinegar, oil and tomato in large bowl.

2 Heat butter in pan; cook asparagus, capsicum and mushrooms, stirring, until asparagus is tender. Add to lamb mixture in bowl; toss gently.

3 Serve lamb mixture with rocket.

serves 4
per serving 27.2g fat; 1698kJ (405 cal)
tip Recipe best made just before serving.

lamb cutlets with white bean salad

PREPARATION TIME 10 MINUTES COOKING TIME 10 MINUTES

12 lamb cutlets (800g)
2 x 300g cans white beans,
   rinsed, drained
3 large egg tomatoes (270g),
   seeded, chopped finely
2 lebanese cucumbers (260g),
   seeded, chopped finely
1 small red onion (100g),
   chopped finely
$^1/_4$ cup (60ml) lemon juice
1 tablespoon wholegrain mustard
$^1/_3$ cup (80ml) olive oil
2 tablespoons coarsely chopped
   fresh flat-leaf parsley

1 Cook lamb, in batches, on heated oiled grill plate (or grill or barbecue) until browned both sides and cooked as desired.

2 Place remaining ingredients in medium bowl; toss to combine. Serve cutlets with white bean salad.

serves 4
per serving 36.1g fat; 2062kJ (492 cal)

korean-style barbecued cutlets

PREPARATION TIME 15 MINUTES COOKING TIME 5 MINUTES

This recipe is an adaptation of the famous Korean barbecued dish bulgogi, where strips of beef are coated in a spicy mixture and barbecued over glowing coals. Today, a variety of meats – including chicken, pork and lamb – are cooked in this manner.

$^1/_2$ **cup (125ml) light soy sauce**
1 cup (250ml) mirin
2 green onions, sliced thinly
2 cloves garlic, crushed
4cm piece fresh ginger (20g), grated finely
1 tablespoon brown sugar
1 tablespoon cracked black pepper
1 tablespoon plain flour
16 lamb cutlets (1kg), trimmed

1 Combine sauce, mirin, onion, garlic, ginger, sugar, pepper and flour in large bowl. Add lamb; toss to coat all over in spice mixture.

2 Cook drained lamb on heated oiled grill plate (or grill or barbecue) until browned both sides and cooked as desired. Brush occasionally with marinade during cooking.

serves 4
per serving 11.7g fat; 1370kJ (328 cal)
tip Lamb can be marinated a day ahead and refrigerated, covered. Traditionally, bulgogi beef was marinated overnight to intensify the flavour.
serving suggestion Serve with steamed jasmine rice and asian greens, such as bok choy, snake beans or snow peas.

balinese-style lamb

PREPARATION TIME 15 MINUTES COOKING TIME 15 MINUTES

Shrimp paste is often sold as trasi or blachan in Asian food stores ... use it sparingly because a little goes a long way!

**5 small fresh red thai chillies,
   seeded, chopped coarsely**
¹/₂ teaspoon shrimp paste
**2 medium brown onions (300g),
   chopped coarsely**
3 cloves garlic, quartered
**10cm piece fresh ginger (50g),
   peeled, chopped coarsely**
**2 tablespoons desiccated coconut,
   toasted**
1 tablespoon peanut oil
1kg lamb fillets, sliced thinly
**1 tablespoon coarsely grated
   palm sugar**
1 tablespoon kecap manis
1 tablespoon dark soy sauce
1 tablespoon lime juice

1 Blend or process chilli, paste, onion, garlic, ginger and coconut until mixture forms a paste.
2 Heat oil in wok or large frying pan; stir-fry lamb, in batches, until browned all over. Add chilli mixture to wok; stir-fry until fragrant.
3 Return lamb to wok with combined remaining ingredients; stir-fry until heated through.

serves 4
per serving 15.8g fat; 1646kJ (394 cal)
tip Brown or black sugar can be used as a substitute for palm sugar.
serving suggestion Serve with steamed jasmine rice and stir-fried snow peas.

iskander kebab

PREPARATION TIME **15 MINUTES** COOKING TIME **15 MINUTES**

1kg lamb rump, cut into 2cm cubes
1 cup (280g) yogurt
2 tablespoons lemon juice
2 cloves garlic, crushed
2 teaspoons finely chopped
  fresh thyme
40g mesclun

CHILLI TOMATO SAUCE
1 tablespoon olive oil
1 small brown onion (80g),
  chopped coarsely
1 clove garlic, crushed
2 long fresh green chillies,
  seeded, chopped coarsely
2 medium tomatoes (380g),
  chopped coarsely
1 tablespoon tomato paste
¹/₃ cup (80ml) dry red wine

1 Thread lamb onto eight skewers. Combine yogurt, juice, garlic and thyme in small bowl. Place two-thirds of the yogurt mixture into separate bowl; reserve. Use remaining yogurt mixture to brush lamb.

2 Cook lamb kebabs, in batches, on heated oiled grill plate (or grill or barbecue) until browned all over and cooked as desired.

3 Serve kebabs with reserved yogurt mixture, chilli tomato sauce and mesclun.
chilli tomato sauce Heat oil in medium frying pan; cook onion and garlic, stirring, until onion softens. Add remaining ingredients; bring to a boil. Reduce heat; simmer, uncovered, about 5 minutes or until sauce thickens slightly. Blend or process sauce until smooth.

serves 4
per serving 25.2g fat; 2116kJ (506 cal)
tip You also can use boned-out leg of lamb, cut into cubes.
serving suggestion Serve kebabs with warm turkish pide.

lamb patties with beetroot and tzatziki

PREPARATION TIME 20 MINUTES COOKING TIME 10 MINUTES

Use the outer leaves of the lettuce for this recipe. The patties and yogurt mixture can be prepared several hours ahead.

500g lamb mince
1 small brown onion (80g), chopped finely
1 medium carrot (120g), grated coarsely
1 egg, beaten lightly
2 tablespoons finely chopped fresh flat-leaf parsley
1 clove garlic, crushed
1 teaspoon grated lemon rind
½ teaspoon dried oregano leaves
½ cup (140g) yogurt
1 clove garlic, crushed, extra
1 lebanese cucumber (130g), seeded, chopped finely
1 tablespoon chopped fresh mint
1 large pide
outer cos lettuce leaves, shredded
400g can whole baby beetroot, drained, quartered

1 Combine lamb, onion, carrot, egg, parsley, garlic, rind and oregano in large bowl; mix well. Shape mixture into 8 patties.
2 Cook patties on heated oiled grill plate or barbecue, in batches, until browned on both sides and cooked as desired.
3 Meanwhile, combine yogurt, extra garlic, cucumber and mint in small bowl; mix well. Cut bread into four even pieces, split each piece in half crossways; toast, cut-side up, until browned lightly.
4 Just before serving, sandwich bread with lettuce leaves, patties, yogurt mixture and beetroot.

serves 4
per serving 14.9g fat; 1240kJ (296 cal)

lamb with sage stir-fry

PREPARATION TIME 15 MINUTES   COOKING TIME 15 MINUTES

500g lamb strips
1 clove garlic, crushed
$1/4$ teaspoon dried crushed chillies
2 tablespoons balsamic vinegar
2 tablespoons olive oil
1 medium yellow capsicum (200g),
    sliced thinly
1 medium red onion (170g),
    sliced thinly
410g can tomatoes
$1/2$ cup (75g) pimiento-stuffed
    green olives
$1^1/2$ tablespoons finely chopped
    fresh sage

1   Combine lamb, garlic, chilli and vinegar in medium bowl.
2   Heat half of the oil in wok or large frying pan. Stir-fry undrained lamb mixture, in batches, until lamb is browned.
3   Heat remaining oil in wok; stir-fry capsicum and onion.
4   Return lamb to wok with undrained crushed tomatoes and remaining ingredients; stir-fry until hot.

serves 4
per serving   15.4g fat; 1209kJ (289 cal)

moroccan lamb with couscous

PREPARATION TIME 15 MINUTES (PLUS STANDING TIME) COOKING TIME 15 MINUTES

Yogurt is used in both the marinade and as the sauce for the lamb in this recipe.

8 lamb fillets (700g)
1 tablespoon ground cumin
1 tablespoon ground coriander
1 teaspoon ground cinnamon
³/₄ cup (200g) yogurt
1¹/₂ cups (300g) couscous
1¹/₂ cups (375ml) boiling water
1 teaspoon peanut oil
¹/₃ cup (50g) dried currants
2 teaspoons finely grated lemon rind
2 teaspoons lemon juice
¹/₄ cup coarsely chopped fresh coriander

1 Combine lamb, spices and ⅓ cup of the yogurt in medium bowl.
2 Cook lamb on heated oiled grill plate (or grill or barbecue) until browned and cooked as desired. Cover; stand 5 minutes, slice thinly.
3 Meanwhile, combine couscous, water and oil in large heatproof bowl, cover; stand 5 minutes or until liquid is absorbed, fluffing with fork occasionally. Stir in currants, rind, juice and coriander; toss with fork to combine.
4 Serve lamb with couscous; drizzle with remaining yogurt.

serves 4
per serving 9.3g fat; 2193kJ (525 cal)
tip Substitute some finely chopped preserved lemon for the lemon juice and rind in the couscous.
Marinate the lamb a day ahead; store, covered, in refrigerator.
serving suggestion Serve with harissa, the fiery North African condiment.

lamb with honeyed garlic vegetables

PREPARATION TIME 15 MINUTES COOKING TIME 20 MINUTES

2 tablespoons peanut oil
400g lamb fillets, sliced thinly
1 clove garlic, crushed
3 finger eggplants (180g), sliced thinly
1 medium white onion (150g), sliced thinly
1 medium carrot (120g), sliced thinly
1 medium red capsicum (200g), sliced thinly
425g can baby corn, drained
100g snow peas
1 tablespoon honey
1 tablespoon cornflour
2 tablespoons oyster sauce
1 tablespoon soy sauce

1 Heat half of the oil in wok or large frying pan. Stir-fry combined lamb and garlic, in batches, until lamb is browned; remove from wok.
2 Heat remaining oil in wok; stir-fry eggplant and onion.
3 Add carrot and capsicum; stir-fry.
4 Add corn and snow peas; stir-fry.
5 Return lamb mixture to wok with honey and blended cornflour and sauces; stir until mixture boils and thickens slightly.

serves 4
per serving 13.7g fat; 1472kJ (352 cal)

tandoori lamb with cucumber raita

PREPARATION TIME 10 MINUTES COOKING TIME 20 MINUTES

8 lamb fillets (700g)
1 tablespoon tandoori paste
1¹/₂ cups (400g) yogurt
1 lebanese cucumber (130g),
  seeded, chopped finely
2 green onions, chopped finely
¹/₂ teaspoon ground cumin
1 teaspoon ground cardamom
2 cups (400g) basmati rice
pinch saffron threads

1 Combine lamb with paste and half of the yogurt in large bowl. Combine remaining yogurt in small bowl with cucumber, onion and half of the combined spices.

2 Place rice and saffron in large saucepan of boiling water; cook, uncovered, until rice is tender. Drain rice; place in large bowl.

3 Toast remaining spices in heated dry small frying pan until fragrant; stir into saffron rice, cover to keep warm.

4 Cook undrained lamb, in batches, on heated lightly oiled grill plate (or grill or barbecue) until browned and cooked as desired.

5 Serve lamb on saffron rice, topped with cucumber raita.

serves 4
per serving 12g fat; 2757kJ (659 cal)
tip You can marinate the lamb a day ahead; store, covered, in refrigerator. Similarly, the cucumber raita can be made several hours ahead; store, covered, in refrigerator.
serving suggestion Serve with a fresh tomato and onion sambal, and pappadums cooked in the microwave oven.

lamb and tabbouleh wrap

PREPARATION TIME 35 MINUTES (PLUS STANDING TIME) COOKING TIME 10 MINUTES

Sumac, a purple-red astringent spice, can be teamed with almost anything – from fish to meat.
It is also great sprinkled over vegetables. You can find sumac at any Middle-Eastern food store.

1 cup (250ml) water
½ cup (80g) burghul
300g can chickpeas, drained, rinsed
⅓ cup (95g) yogurt
1 teaspoon finely grated lemon rind
1 tablespoon lemon juice
3 green onions, sliced thinly
2 medium tomatoes (380g), seeded,
   chopped finely
1 lebanese cucumber (130g), seeded,
   chopped finely
1 cup coarsely chopped fresh
   flat-leaf parsley
½ cup coarsely chopped fresh mint
1 tablespoon lemon juice, extra
300g lamb strips
2 tablespoons sumac
8 slices lavash bread

1 Combine the water and burghul in small bowl; stand 30 minutes.
   Drain; squeeze burghul with hands to remove excess water.

2 Meanwhile, blend or process chickpeas, yogurt, rind and juice until
   hummus is smooth.

3 Combine burghul in large bowl with onion, tomato, cucumber and
   herbs; add extra juice, toss gently until tabbouleh is combined.

4 Toss lamb in sumac; cook, in batches, on heated lightly oiled grill plate
   (or grill or barbecue) until browned both sides and cooked as desired.

5 Just before serving, spread hummus equally over half of each slice of the
   bread, top with equal amounts of lamb and tabbouleh; roll to enclose filling.
   Cut into pieces, if desired, to serve.

makes 8 wraps
per wrap 3.8g fat; 1244kJ (297 cal)

pork rice-paper rolls

PREPARATION TIME 30 MINUTES COOKING TIME 10 MINUTES

*When soaked in hot water, vietnamese rice-paper sheets (banh trang)
make pliable wrappers for a host of fillings. You will need a small
chinese cabbage for this recipe.*

**350g pork mince
1 clove garlic, crushed
1cm piece fresh ginger (5g), grated finely
1 teaspoon five-spice powder
350g finely shredded chinese cabbage
4 green onions, sliced thinly
1 tablespoon soy sauce
1/4 cup (60ml) oyster sauce
1/4 cup coarsely chopped fresh coriander
12 x 22cm rice paper sheets
1/4 cup (60ml) sweet chilli sauce
2 tablespoons lime juice**

1 Cook pork, garlic, ginger and spice in large non-stick frying pan,
   stirring, until pork is changed in colour and cooked through.
2 Add cabbage, onion, soy sauce, oyster sauce and 2 tablespoons
   of the coriander to pan; cook, stirring, until cabbage is just wilted.
3 Place one sheet of rice paper in medium bowl of warm water until
   softened slightly; lift sheet carefully from water, place on board, pat
   dry with absorbent paper. Place a twelfth of the filling mixture in centre
   of sheet; fold in sides, roll top to bottom to enclose filling. Repeat with
   remaining rice paper sheets and filling.
4 Place rolls in single layer in large steamer set over large saucepan of
   simmering water; steam, covered, about 5 minutes or until just heated
   through. Serve rolls with dipping sauce made with combined remaining
   coriander, sweet chilli sauce and juice.

serves 4
per serving 7.1g fat; 1041kJ (249 cal)
tip Rolls can be prepared a day ahead; store, covered, in refrigerator.

honey and soy roast pork

PREPARATION TIME 10 MINUTES   COOKING TIME 30 MINUTES

2 medium pork fillets (700g)
750g kumara, sliced thickly
1 tablespoon wholegrain mustard
2 tablespoons honey
1 tablespoon soy sauce
4 green onions, sliced thinly

1 Preheat oven to very hot.
2 Place pork and kumara in oiled baking dish.
3 Pour over combined mustard, honey and soy sauce; toss to coat pork and kumara in honey mixture.
4 Cook pork and kumara, uncovered, in very hot oven about 30 minutes or until they are cooked through.
5 Slice pork; serve with kumara. Top with green onion; drizzle with pan juices. Accompany with steamed sugar snap peas, if desired.

serves 4
per serving 3g fat; 1391kJ (332 cal)
tip Pork can be marinated in half of the mustard mixture overnight.

pork and broccolini stir-fry

PREPARATION TIME 15 MINUTES   COOKING TIME 20 MINUTES

2 tablespoons peanut oil
450g pork steaks, sliced thinly
1 medium red onion (170g),
   sliced thinly
1 medium red capsicum (200g),
   sliced thinly
1 clove garlic, crushed
1cm piece fresh ginger (5g),
   grated finely
300g broccolini
1 teaspoon cornflour
2 tablespoons lemon juice
¹/₄ cup (60ml) water
¹/₄ cup (60ml) sweet chilli sauce
1 teaspoon fish sauce
1 tablespoon light soy sauce
1 teaspoon sesame oil
1 tablespoon coarsely chopped
   fresh coriander
1 tablespoon coarsely chopped
   fresh mint

1   Heat half of the peanut oil in wok or large frying pan; stir-fry pork, in batches, until browned.
2   Heat remaining peanut oil in wok; stir-fry onion, capsicum, garlic and ginger until vegetables are just tender.
3   Meanwhile, trim and halve broccolini. Blend cornflour with juice in small bowl; add the water, sauces and sesame oil. Stir mixture to combine.
4   Return pork to wok with broccolini and cornflour mixture; stir-fry about 2 minutes or until mixture boils and thickens slightly. Remove from heat; stir in coriander and mint just before serving.

serves 4
per serving 15g fat; 1234kJ (295 cal)

pork and sage with fettuccine

PREPARATION TIME 15 MINUTES COOKING TIME 15 MINUTES

1 tablespoon olive oil
100g shaved ham
2 tablespoons fresh sage leaves
8 pork schnitzels (800g)
1 cup (250ml) dry white wine
1 tablespoon brown sugar
250g fettuccine
150g baby spinach leaves
1 small red onion (100g), sliced thinly
2 tablespoons finely chopped fresh chives
1 tablespoon extra virgin olive oil

1 Heat half of the olive oil in large frying pan; cook ham, stirring, until browned lightly. Remove from pan; cover to keep warm.
2 Cook sage in same pan, stirring, until just wilted. Remove from pan; cover to keep warm.
3 Heat remaining olive oil in same pan; cook pork, uncovered, until browned both sides and just cooked through. Remove from pan; cover to keep warm.
4 Combine wine and sugar in same pan; boil, uncovered, until sauce reduces by a third.
5 Meanwhile, cook pasta in large saucepan of boiling water, uncovered, until just tender; drain, reserving ½ cup of the cooking liquid.
6 Place pasta and reserved hot cooking liquid in large bowl with spinach, onion, chives and extra virgin olive oil; toss gently to combine. Top pasta mixture with pork, ham and sage; drizzle with sauce.

serves 4
per serving 16g fat; 2555kJ (610 cal)

rice noodle and pork stir-fry

PREPARATION TIME 10 MINUTES COOKING TIME 10 MINUTES

375g packet rice stick noodles
2 tablespoons vegetable oil
2 eggs, beaten lightly
400g pork and veal mince
2 small fresh red thai chillies,
    seeded, chopped
2 cloves garlic, crushed
1cm piece fresh ginger (5g), grated finely
1¹/₂ tablespoons fish sauce
1¹/₂ tablespoons lime juice
¹/₃ cup (80ml) kecap manis
6 green onions, sliced
1 cup (80g) bean sprouts
¹/₃ cup chopped fresh coriander
2 tablespoons coarsely chopped
    toasted peanuts

1 Add noodles to large saucepan of boiling water; boil, uncovered, about 2 minutes or until noodles are tender. Drain.
2 Meanwhile, heat 2 teaspoons of the oil in wok or large frying pan, add egg, swirl wok to make thin omelette. Remove from wok, roll up and slice thinly.
3 Heat remaining oil in wok, add mince in batches, stir-fry until browned; remove from wok.
4 Add chilli, garlic and ginger to wok, stir-fry until fragrant.
5 Add fish sauce, juice, kecap manis, noodles, mince, onion and sprouts to wok, stir-fry until noodles are heated through. Add coriander and omelette, toss gently.
6 Serve sprinkled with peanuts.

serves 4
per serving 22g fat; 1729kJ (413 cal)

marmalade-glazed pork cutlets

PREPARATION TIME 5 MINUTES COOKING TIME 20 MINUTES

$1/2$ **cup (125ml) dry red wine**
$1/3$ **cup (115g) orange marmalade**
1 clove garlic, crushed
$1/3$ **cup (80ml) fresh orange juice**
1 tablespoon olive oil
4 pork cutlets (940g)

1 Combine wine, marmalade, garlic and juice in small saucepan; bring to a boil. Remove from heat.
2 Heat oil in large frying pan; cook pork until browned both sides and cooked through, brushing constantly with marmalade glaze.

serves 4
per serving 10.2g fat; 1331kJ (318 cal)
serving suggestion Serve with steamed rice and stir-fried baby bok choy or choy sum.

teriyaki pork with wasabi dressing

PREPARATION TIME 10 MINUTES   COOKING TIME 15 MINUTES

750g pork fillets
$^1/_4$ cup (60ml) teriyaki marinade
50g snow pea sprouts
100g mesclun
50g watercress, trimmed
1 medium red capsicum (200g), sliced thinly
250g yellow teardrop tomatoes, halved

WASABI DRESSING
$1^1/_2$ teaspoons wasabi powder
$^1/_4$ cup (60ml) cider vinegar
$^1/_3$ cup (80ml) vegetable oil
1 tablespoon light soy sauce

1 Trim pork; brush with teriyaki marinade. Cook pork, in batches, on heated oiled grill plate (or grill or barbecue), brushing frequently with marinade, until browned both sides and cooked. Cover to keep warm.

2 Meanwhile, combine sprouts, mesclun, watercress, capsicum and tomato in large bowl.

3 Pour wasabi dressing over salad mixture; toss gently to combine. Slice pork; serve with salad.

wasabi dressing Blend wasabi powder with vinegar in small jug; whisk in remaining ingredients.

serves 4
per serving 23g fat; 1799kJ (430 cal)

salt and pepper prawns

Shell and devein uncooked king prawns, leaving the tails intact. Combine sea salt, five-spice powder and freshly ground black pepper; sprinkle the salt mixture all over prawns. Cook prawns on heated oiled barbecue until cooked through.

scallops with garlic and caper butter

Melt butter in small saucepan, add crushed garlic, drained and chopped capers and chopped fresh oregano. Cook scallops on heated oiled barbecue until browned on one side; turn, spoon over some of the butter mixture. Cook until just cooked through. Serve with remaining butter mixture.

chicken tikka

Combine chicken tenderloins with prepared tikka paste. Cook chicken on heated oiled barbecue until browned all over and cooked through. Serve chicken with combined yogurt, chopped fresh mint, a pinch of ground cumin and a peeled, seeded and finely chopped lebanese cucumber.

lamb cutlets with beetroot yogurt dip

Blend or process drained, canned sliced beetroot with yogurt, chopped fresh coriander and crushed garlic. Cook lamb cutlets on a heated oiled barbecue until cooked through. Serve the beetroot dip with barbecued lamb cutlets.

pesto chicken

Combine basil pesto and a little balsamic vinegar in small bowl. Brush mixture over chicken breast fillets. Cook chicken on heated oiled barbecue until browned both sides and cooked through. Stand 5 minutes before slicing. Serve on a bed of mesclun, drizzled with olive oil.

fish kebabs

Cut firm white fish fillets into 2cm pieces. Combine fish with chopped fresh mint, coriander, parsley, lime juice, crushed garlic, grated fresh ginger and a little peanut oil. Thread fish onto skewers. Cook skewers on heated oiled barbecue until browned all over and cooked through.

chilli garlic octopus

Combine cleaned baby octopus with olive oil, crushed garlic, lemon juice and sweet chilli sauce. Cook the octopus on a heated oiled barbecue until browned all over and cooked through. Serve octopus with lime wedges, if desired.

beef steaks with green capsicum salsa

Combine finely chopped green capsicum, red onion, red thai chilli, green onion, lime juice, mint and a pinch of sugar. Serve salsa with barbecued beef steaks.

pasta & noodles

Nothing is faster to cook than fresh pasta or noodles. As part of a stir-fry, or as the main ingredient in a pasta meal, these are two of the easiest and fastest dishes to prepare. So, when you're in a hurry, try a crispy noodle salad, chilli pork noodles or bucatini with baked ricotta.

singapore noodles

PREPARATION TIME 10 MINUTES   COOKING TIME 20 MINUTES

250g rice vermicelli
4 eggs, beaten lightly
2 teaspoons vegetable oil
1 medium brown onion (150g),
   chopped coarsely
2 cloves garlic, crushed
2cm piece fresh ginger (10g), grated finely
150g baby bok choy, chopped coarsely
200g snow peas, halved
1 small red capsicum (150g), sliced thickly
2 tablespoons soy sauce
2 tablespoons oyster sauce
2 tablespoons sweet chilli sauce
1 cup loosely packed fresh
   coriander leaves
3 cups bean sprouts (240g)

1 Place noodles in large heatproof bowl, cover with boiling water, stand until just tender; drain. Using scissors, cut noodles into 10cm lengths.
2 Heat lightly oiled wok or large frying pan; add half of the egg, swirling wok to form thin omelette. Remove omelette from wok; roll into cigar shape, cut into thin slices. Repeat with remaining egg.
3 Heat oil in wok; stir-fry onion until soft. Add garlic and ginger; cook, stirring, 1 minute. Add bok choy, snow peas, capsicum and sauces; cook, stirring, until vegetables are just tender.
4 Add noodles and egg strips with coriander and sprouts to wok; toss gently to combine.

serves 4
per serving 9.9g fat; 1545kJ (369 cal)

chicken stir-fry on noodle cakes

PREPARATION TIME 10 MINUTES COOKING TIME 10 MINUTES

**3 x 85g packets chicken-flavoured
instant noodles**
2 tablespoons peanut oil
700g chicken breast fillets, sliced thinly
**1 small brown onion (100g),
sliced thinly**
1 clove garlic, crushed
1 medium carrot (120g), sliced thinly
**1 large red capsicum (350g),
sliced thinly**
400g baby bok choy, quartered
**2cm piece fresh ginger (10g),
grated finely**
⅓ cup (80ml) oyster sauce
2 tablespoons soy sauce
¾ cup (180ml) chicken stock
1 tablespoon cornflour

1 Cook noodles following the instructions on packet. Drain noodles, add one of the flavour sachets and stir to combine (reserve remaining sachets for another use). Heat half of the oil in large frying pan, add noodles and press into a "cake" shape. Cook until browned on both sides.
2 Meanwhile, heat remaining oil in wok or large frying pan; stir-fry chicken, in batches, until cooked through.
3 Add onion and garlic to wok; stir-fry until just tender. Add carrot and capsicum; stir-fry until just tender.
4 Return chicken to wok with bok choy and combined ginger, sauces, stock and cornflour; stir-fry until mixture boils and thickens.
5 Cut noodle cake into quarters. Serve stir-fry on noodle cakes.

serves 4
per serving 20.7g fat; 1988kJ (476 cal)

sweet soy chicken with noodles

PREPARATION TIME 10 MINUTES COOKING TIME 20 MINUTES

We used hokkien noodles in this recipe, but any fresh wheat noodle such as shanghai can be substituted.

500g hokkien noodles
1 tablespoon peanut oil
750g chicken thigh fillets, sliced thickly
8 green onions, chopped coarsely
4 cloves garlic, crushed
2cm piece fresh ginger (10g), sliced thinly
230g can sliced water chestnuts, drained
300g choy sum, trimmed, chopped coarsely
2 tablespoons coarsely chopped fresh coriander
2 tablespoons kecap manis
$1/4$ cup (60ml) chicken stock

1 Rinse noodles in strainer under hot water. Separate noodles with fork; drain.
2 Heat oil in wok or large frying pan; stir-fry chicken, in batches, until browned all over and cooked through. Return chicken to wok with onion, garlic, ginger and water chestnuts; stir-fry until fragrant. Add choy sum, coriander, kecap manis and stock; stir-fry until choy sum just wilts.
3 Top noodles with chicken. Serve with sambal oelek, if desired.

serves 4
per serving 19.1g fat; 2030kJ (486 cal)
tips Use chinese broccoli if choy sum is unavailable.

snow pea and asian-green stir-fry

PREPARATION TIME 10 MINUTES COOKING TIME 10 MINUTES

You can vary the asian greens in this recipe according to what's available at the greengrocer.

375g dried rice noodles
1 tablespoon peanut oil
1 medium brown onion (150g),
**   sliced thinly**
1 clove garlic, crushed
2cm piece fresh ginger (10g), grated finely
4 baby bok choy (600g), trimmed,
**   halved lengthways**
250g choy sum, trimmed
250g chinese broccoli, chopped coarsely
200g snow peas, halved
2 tablespoons light soy sauce
¼ cup (60ml) hoisin sauce
¼ cup (60ml) plum sauce
¼ cup (60ml) vegetable stock
2 teaspoons sesame oil
1 tablespoon white sesame seeds, toasted

1 Place noodles in medium heatproof bowl, cover with boiling water, stand until just tender; drain.

2 Heat peanut oil in wok or large frying pan; stir-fry onion, garlic and ginger until onion softens.

3 Add bok choy, choy sum, broccoli and snow peas with combined sauces, stock and sesame oil; stir-fry until greens are just tender.

4 Serve stir-fry on noodles; sprinkle with seeds.

serves 4
per serving 11.1g fat; 1995kJ (477 cal)
tips Add tofu to the stir-fry to boost the protein content. Substitute your favourite noodles for the rice noodles, if you prefer.

serving suggestion Serve with chopped chilli if you like your noodles spicy.

linguine with asparagus and chilli pancetta

PREPARATION TIME 20 MINUTES   COOKING TIME 20 MINUTES

500g linguine
150g thinly sliced chilli pancetta, halved
¹/₃ cup (80ml) extra virgin olive oil
2 cloves garlic, sliced thinly
250g asparagus, trimmed, sliced thinly
100g baby rocket leaves
¼ cup (60ml) lemon juice

1 Cook pasta in large saucepan of boiling water, uncovered, until just tender; drain.
2 Meanwhile, cook pancetta, in batches, in large non-stick frying pan until browned both sides and crisp. Remove pancetta from the pan and keep warm. Add oil, garlic and asparagus to same pan; cook, until fragrant.
3 Return drained pasta to saucepan and pour over hot asparagus mixture, rocket and juice. Stir through crisp pancetta.

serves 4
per serving 25g fat; 2866kJ (685 cal)

ravioli salad

PREPARATION TIME 15 MINUTES COOKING TIME 15 MINUTES

You need approximately 500g fresh broccoli for this recipe, and you can use any variety of ravioli you like.

375g spinach and ricotta ravioli
4 bacon rashers (280g), chopped coarsely
250g (2 cups) broccoli florets
250g cherry tomatoes, halved
2 tablespoons finely shredded fresh basil
$^1/_2$ cup (125ml) olive oil
$^1/_4$ cup (60ml) white wine vinegar
2 tablespoons sun-dried tomato pesto

1 Cook pasta in large saucepan of boiling water, uncovered, until just tender; drain. Rinse under cold water; drain.
2 Meanwhile, cook bacon in small frying pan, stirring, until browned and crisp; drain on absorbent paper.
3 Boil, steam or microwave broccoli until just tender, drain. Rinse under cold water; drain.
4 Place ravioli, bacon and broccoli in large bowl with tomato, basil and combined remaining ingredients; toss gently to combine.

serves 4
per serving 37.9g fat; 2205kJ (528 cal)
tip You can use any kind of prepared pesto you prefer in this salad's dressing: roasted vegetable is a good alternative.
per serving This salad can serve as the main course for a light lunch or late supper, accompanied by a simple green salad and a loaf of fresh bread.

soy chicken and vegetable noodle stir-fry

PREPARATION TIME 15 MINUTES (PLUS STANDING TIME)   COOKING TIME 20 MINUTES

600g chicken breast fillets, sliced thickly
2 cloves garlic, crushed
¹/₃ cup (80ml) soy sauce
¹/₃ cup (80ml) oyster sauce
400g fresh rice noodles
2 tablespoons peanut oil
1 medium brown onion (150g), sliced thinly
200g broccoli, cut into florets
200g baby corn, halved lengthways
1 medium red capsicum (200g), sliced thinly
2 small green zucchini (180g), sliced thinly
¹/₃ cup (80ml) chicken stock
200g snow peas, sliced thickly
150g bean sprouts
4 green onions, chopped coarsely

1 Combine chicken, garlic and 2 tablespoons each of the soy and oyster sauces in large bowl.
2 Place noodles in large heatproof bowl; cover with boiling water. Stand 5 minutes; drain.
3 Heat half of the oil in wok or large frying pan. Stir-fry undrained chicken, in batches, until browned all over and cooked through; remove from wok.
4 Heat remaining oil in wok; stir-fry brown onion until soft.
5 Add broccoli, corn, capsicum and zucchini; stir-fry until vegetables are just tender.
6 Return chicken to wok with combined remaining sauces and stock; stir-fry until sauce boils.
7 Remove wok from heat; add noodles, snow peas, bean sprouts and green onion.

serves 6
per serving 9.6g fat; 1366kJ (326 cal)
tip Chicken thigh fillets can be substituted.

greek lamb, fetta and eggplant pasta

PREPARATION TIME 20 MINUTES (PLUS STANDING TIME) COOKING TIME 15 MINUTES

1 medium eggplant (300g),
   chopped coarsely
cooking salt
500g lamb fillets
2 tablespoons olive oil
250g large pasta shells
1 medium red onion (170g),
   sliced thinly
100g baby rocket leaves
2 medium tomatoes (380g),
   seeded, sliced thinly
¹/₄ cup loosely packed fresh
   oregano leaves
200g fetta cheese, crumbled

BALSAMIC VINAIGRETTE
¹/₄ cup (60ml) balsamic vinegar
¹/₂ cup (125ml) olive oil
2 cloves garlic, crushed
2 tablespoons wholegrain mustard

1 Place eggplant in colander, sprinkle all over with salt. Stand 5 minutes; rinse under cold water, drain on absorbent paper.
2 Meanwhile, cook lamb, in batches, in large non-stick frying pan until browned and cooked as desired. Stand 5 minutes; cut into thick slices.
3 Heat oil in same pan; cook eggplant, in batches, until browned all over and tender.
4 Meanwhile, cook pasta in large saucepan of boiling water, uncovered, until just tender; drain.
5 Place pasta, lamb and eggplant in large bowl with remaining ingredients; drizzle with balsamic vinaigrette, toss gently to combine.
   balsamic vinaigrette Combine ingredients in screw-top jar; shake well.

serves 4
per serving 55.1g fat; 3636kJ (870 cal)

sesame beef and noodles

PREPARATION TIME 15 MINUTES COOKING TIME 10 MINUTES

500g beef steak, sliced thinly
1 tablespoon peanut oil
1 teaspoon sesame oil
2 cloves garlic, crushed
750g fresh rice noodle sheets
300g broccoli, chopped coarsely
2 tablespoons sesame seeds
$^1/_4$ cup (60ml) oyster sauce
$^1/_4$ cup (60ml) mild sweet chilli sauce

1 Combine beef, oils and garlic in medium bowl.
2 Separate noodle sheets; cut into 2cm strips.
3 Boil, steam or microwave broccoli until just tender; drain.
4 Stir-fry beef mixture in heated wok or large frying pan,
   in batches, until beef is browned.
5 Stir-fry seeds until they pop.
6 Return beef to wok with noodles, broccoli and sauces;
   stir-fry until hot.

serves 4
per serving 18.9g fat; 2099kJ (501 cal)

penne, roast capsicum and baby vegetables in burnt butter sauce

PREPARATION TIME 15 MINUTES (PLUS STANDING TIME) COOKING TIME 20 MINUTES

2 medium red capsicums (400g)
375g penne
200g baby corn, halved lengthways
200g green beans, trimmed
100g butter
2 cloves garlic, crushed
2 tablespoons coarsely chopped
   fresh oregano

1 Quarter capsicums, remove and discard seeds and membranes. Roast under grill or in very hot oven, skin-side up, until skin blisters and blackens. Cover capsicum pieces with plastic or paper for 5 minutes, peel away skin, slice capsicum thinly.

2 Cook pasta in large saucepan of boiling water, uncovered, until just tender; drain.

3 Meanwhile, boil, steam or microwave corn and beans, separately, until just tender; drain.

4 Melt butter in small saucepan; cook, stirring, about 3 minutes or until browned. Remove from heat; stir in garlic and oregano.

5 Place pasta in large bowl with corn, beans, capsicum and herbed burnt butter; toss gently to combine.

serves 4
per serving 22.4g fat; 2400kJ (574 cal)
tips Basil can be substituted for the oregano.
Capsicum can be roasted the day ahead and kept, covered, in the refrigerator.

chilli pork noodles

PREPARATION TIME 10 MINUTES COOKING TIME 10 MINUTES

Udon, wide Japanese noodles made from wheat flour, are available fresh or dried from Asian supermarkets. You can substitute any dried flat wheat noodle, but check the manufacturer's instructions regarding their preparation.

500g udon
1 tablespoon peanut oil
2 tablespoons finely chopped garlic chives
3 cloves garlic, crushed
3 small fresh red thai chillies, seeded, chopped finely
500g pork mince
¼ cup (60ml) light soy sauce
½ cup (125ml) chicken stock
1 cup (80g) bean sprouts
4 green onions, sliced thinly

1 Cook noodles in large saucepan of boiling water, uncovered, until just tender; drain.
2 Meanwhile, heat oil in wok or large frying pan; stir-fry chives, garlic and chilli until fragrant.
3 Add pork; stir-fry until cooked through. Add sauce and stock; stir-fry until hot.
4 Serve pork mixture on noodles; top with sprouts and onion.

serves 4
per serving 14.8g fat; 1789kJ (430 cal)
tip Dried udon are available in different thicknesses, so the cooking time will vary depending on the size.
serving suggestion Serve these noodles with asian greens in oyster sauce.

vegetarian pad thai

PREPARATION TIME 15 MINUTES (PLUS STANDING TIME)
COOKING TIME 10 MINUTES

200g rice stick noodles
¼ cup (60ml) peanut oil
2 eggs, beaten lightly
2 cloves garlic, crushed
2 small fresh red thai chillies, seeded, chopped finely
1 cup (90g) fried onion
125g fried tofu, cut into small pieces
¼ cup (35g) coarsely chopped roasted unsalted peanuts
3 cups (240g) bean sprouts
6 green onions, sliced thinly
2 tablespoons soy sauce
1 tablespoon lime juice
2 tablespoons coarsely chopped fresh coriander

1 Place noodles in large heatproof bowl; cover with boiling water, stand until noodles just soften, drain.
2 Heat 2 teaspoons of the oil in wok; pour in egg, swirl wok to make thin omelette. Cook, uncovered, until egg is just set. Remove from wok; roll omelette, cut into thin strips.
3 Heat remaining oil in wok; stir-fry garlic, chilli and fried onion until fragrant. Add tofu; stir-fry 1 minute. Add half of the nuts, half of the sprouts and half of the green onion; stir-fry until sprouts are just wilted. Add noodles, sauce and juice; stir-fry, tossing gently until combined.
4 Remove from heat; toss remaining nuts, sprouts and green onion with omelette strips and coriander through pad thai.

serves 4
per serving 27g fat; 1813kJ (433 cal)

crispy noodle salad

PREPARATION TIME 15 MINUTES

Crispy fried noodles are sold packaged (usually in a 100g packet), already deep-fried and ready to eat.
They are sometimes labelled crunchy noodles, and are available in two widths — thin and spaghetti-like
or wide and flat, like fettuccine; we used the thin variety in this recipe.

1 medium red capsicum (200g)
100g baby curly endive
100g crispy fried noodles
1 small red onion (100g), sliced thinly
1 tablespoon coarsely chopped
    fresh mint
1 tablespoon coarsely chopped
    fresh coriander

DRESSING
$^1/_3$ cup (80ml) peanut oil
1 tablespoon white vinegar
1 tablespoon brown sugar
1 tablespoon light soy sauce
1 teaspoon sesame oil
1 clove garlic, crushed

1 Cut capsicum in half lengthways. Remove and discard seeds and membranes; slice capsicum pieces thinly. Trim endive; discard hard ends of leaves.
2 Combine capsicum and endive with noodles, onion, mint and coriander in large bowl. Add dressing; toss to combine.
   dressing Combine ingredients in screw-top jar; shake well.

serves 4
per serving 22.7g fat; 1104kJ (264 cal)

satay beef stir-fry with hokkien noodles

PREPARATION TIME 15 MINUTES COOKING TIME 15 MINUTES

600g hokkien noodles
300g beef rump steak, sliced thinly
$^1/_2$cm piece fresh ginger (2.5g),
   grated finely
2 teaspoons sesame oil
1 small red onion (100g), sliced thinly
1 medium red capsicum (200g),
   sliced thinly
150g broccoli florets
2 teaspoons lime juice
$^1/_4$ cup (60ml) satay sauce
1 tablespoon hoisin sauce
$^1/_3$ cup (80ml) soy sauce
1 tablespoon kecap manis
150g snow peas
1 tablespoon finely chopped
   fresh coriander
$^1/_4$ cup (35g) unsalted roasted
   peanuts, chopped coarsely

1 Place noodles in large heatproof bowl, cover with boiling water; separate with fork, drain.
2 Heat oiled wok or large non-stick frying pan; stir-fry beef and ginger, in batches, until browned.
3 Heat oil in wok; stir-fry onion, capsicum and broccoli until just tender. Return beef to wok with combined juice and sauces; stir-fry until sauce boils. Add noodles and snow peas; stir-fry until hot.
4 Add coriander; stir-fry until combined. Serve sprinkled with peanuts.

serves 4
per serving 15.8g fat; 2788kJ (667 cal)
serving suggestion Serve with a bowl of sambal oelek, the fiery-hot indonesian chilli and vinegar sauce.

hokkien noodles with prawns

PREPARATION TIME **20 MINUTES**   COOKING TIME **10 MINUTES**

1.2kg large uncooked prawns
500g hokkien noodles
300g baby bok choy
2 teaspoons peanut oil
1 small fresh red thai chilli, chopped finely
1 clove garlic, crushed
$^1/_4$ cup (60ml) water
2 tablespoons sesame oil
$^1/_2$ cup (125ml) kecap manis
$^1/_4$ cup (60ml) light soy sauce
$^1/_2$ cup coarsely chopped fresh coriander

1 Shell and devein prawns, leaving tails intact.
2 Place noodles in large heatproof bowl, cover with boiling water; separate with fork, drain. Cut bok choy into quarters lengthways.
3 Heat half of the peanut oil in wok or large frying pan; stir-fry chilli and garlic briefly, until just fragrant. Add prawns, in batches; stir-fry over high heat until just changed in colour.
4 Heat remaining peanut oil in wok; stir-fry noodles and bok choy over high heat until bok choy just wilts.
5 Return prawns to wok with the water, sesame oil, kecap manis, sauce and coriander; stir-fry briefly over high heat until prawn mixture is just hot.

serves 4
per serving 12.9g fat; 1716kJ (411 cal)

rice noodle salad

PREPARATION TIME 20 MINUTES (PLUS STANDING TIME)

150g rice stick noodles
$^1/_4$ cup (60ml) lime juice
$^1/_4$ cup (60ml) sweet chilli sauce
1 tablespoon light soy sauce
1 tablespoon sugar
6 cups (480g) finely shredded
 red cabbage
1 large carrot (180g), sliced thinly
1 lebanese cucumber (130g), seeded,
 sliced thinly
3 medium egg tomatoes (225g),
 seeded, sliced thinly
1 medium yellow capsicum (200g),
 sliced thinly
$^1/_2$ cup firmly packed fresh
 coriander leaves
$^1/_2$ cup firmly packed fresh mint leaves
$^1/_2$ cup firmly packed fresh thai
 basil leaves

1 Place noodles in large heatproof bowl, cover with boiling water; stand until just tender, drain.
2 Meanwhile, combine juice, sauces and sugar in small bowl; stir until sugar dissolves.
3 Place noodles in large bowl with juice mixture and remaining ingredients; toss to combine thoroughly.

serves 4
per serving 1.6g fat; 903kJ (216 cal)

bow ties with zucchini in lemon garlic sauce

PREPARATION TIME 10 MINUTES   COOKING TIME 20 MINUTES

375g bow tie pasta
3 medium yellow zucchini (360g)
3 medium green zucchini (360g)
30g butter
1 tablespoon olive oil
2 cloves garlic, crushed
$^1/_3$ cup (80ml) vegetable stock
$^1/_2$ cup (125ml) cream
2 teaspoons finely grated lemon rind
$^1/_3$ cup coarsely chopped fresh chives

1 Cook pasta in large saucepan of boiling water, uncovered, until just tender; drain.
2 Meanwhile, halve zucchini lengthways; slice halves thinly on the diagonal.
3 Heat butter and oil in large frying pan; cook zucchini and garlic over high heat, stirring, until zucchini is just tender. Add stock; bring to a boil. Reduce heat, add cream, rind and chives; stir until hot.
4 Place pasta in pan with zucchini sauce; toss gently to combine.

serves 4
per serving 26.1g fat; 2356kJ (564 cal)

seafood salad

PREPARATION TIME 5 MINUTES (PLUS REFRIGERATION TIME)
COOKING TIME 20 MINUTES

1 teaspoon olive oil
1 small brown onion (80g), sliced thinly
1 clove garlic, crushed
500g seafood marinara mix
375g large pasta shells
1 tablespoon dry white wine
$^1/_2$ cup (150g) mayonnaise
1 teaspoon lemon juice
2 teaspoons worcestershire sauce
$^1/_3$ cup (80ml) tomato sauce
$^1/_4$ teaspoon Tabasco sauce
1 tablespoon coarsely chopped fresh flat-leaf parsley
100g baby rocket leaves

1 Heat oil in large frying pan; cook onion and garlic, stirring, until onion softens. Add marinara mix; cook, stirring, until seafood is cooked through. Place marinara mixture in large bowl, cover; refrigerate until cold.

2 Meanwhile, cook pasta in large saucepan of boiling water, uncovered, until just tender; drain. Rinse under cold water; drain.

3 Place pasta and combined wine, mayonnaise, juice, sauces and parsley in bowl with marinara mixture; toss gently to combine. Serve seafood salad on rocket leaves.

serves 4
per serving 15.2g fat; 2650kJ (634 cal)

creamy lamb and linguine with mint pesto

PREPARATION TIME 15 MINUTES COOKING TIME 25 MINUTES

500g linguine
2 cups firmly packed
**   fresh mint leaves**
2 cloves garlic, crushed
¹/₃ cup (50g) pine nuts
2 tablespoons grated
**   parmesan cheese**
¹/₃ cup (80ml) light olive oil
500g lamb fillets, sliced thinly
300ml cream

1   Cook linguine in large saucepan of boiling
    water, uncovered, until just tender; drain.
2   Process mint, garlic, pine nuts, cheese
    and ¼ cup (60ml) of the oil until combined.
3   Heat remaining oil in wok or large frying pan.
    Stir-fry lamb, in batches, until browned.
4   Combine mint pesto and cream in wok; stir well.
5   Return lamb and linguine to wok; stir-fry until hot.

serves 4
per serving 61.8g fat; 4704kJ (1124 cal)

scallops and snow peas with noodles

PREPARATION TIME 15 MINUTES   COOKING TIME 15 MINUTES

¹/₃ cup (75g) sugar
¹/₃ cup (80ml) water
¹/₂ cup (125ml) lime juice
2 tablespoons oyster sauce
1 clove garlic, crushed
250g thin fresh egg noodles
1 tablespoon peanut oil
¹/₂ teaspoon sesame oil
600g scallops
1 medium carrot (120g),
   cut into thin strips
8 green onions, sliced thinly
150g snow peas
2 tablespoons finely chopped
   fresh coriander

1 Combine sugar, the water and juice in small saucepan. Cook, stirring, without boiling, until sugar is dissolved; bring to a boil. Boil, uncovered, 3 minutes; stir in sauce and garlic.
2 Cook noodles in large saucepan of boiling water, uncovered, until just tender; drain.
3 Heat oils in wok or large frying pan. Stir-fry scallops, in batches, until just tender.
4 Stir-fry carrot, onion and peas.
5 Return scallops to wok. Add lime mixture; stir until hot.
6 Serve scallop mixture over noodles, sprinkled with coriander.

serves 4
per serving 7.2g fat; 1691kJ (404 cal)

rag pasta with pumpkin and sage

PREPARATION TIME 15 MINUTES   COOKING TIME 15 MINUTES

500g lasagne sheets
50g butter
¼ cup (60ml) extra virgin olive oil
1kg butternut pumpkin, sliced thinly
2 cloves garlic, sliced thinly
1 teaspoon fresh thyme leaves
½ cup (40g) grated parmesan cheese
2 teaspoons fresh sage leaves

1 Break lasagne sheets into large pieces. Cook lasagne in large saucepan of boiling water until just tender. Drain, reserving 2 tablespoons of the cooking liquid.
2 Meanwhile, heat butter and oil in large non-stick frying pan, add pumpkin; cook, stirring gently, until pumpkin is just tender. Add garlic and thyme; cook, stirring, until fragrant.
3 Just before serving, add cheese and sage; gently toss through pasta with the reserved cooking liquid. Sprinkle with extra parmesan cheese flakes, if desired.

serves 4
per serving 29.7g fat; 3173kJ (758 cal)

bucatini with baked ricotta

PREPARATION TIME 5 MINUTES COOKING TIME 15 MINUTES

375g bucatini
2 x 270g jars marinated eggplant in oil
2 cloves garlic, crushed
2 x 410g cans tomatoes
¹/₂ teaspoon cracked black pepper
300g baked ricotta, chopped coarsely

1   Cook pasta in large saucepan of boiling water, uncovered, until just tender; drain.
2   Meanwhile, cook undrained eggplant and garlic in large saucepan, stirring, until fragrant.
3   Stir pasta, undrained crushed tomatoes and pepper into eggplant mixture; toss over medium heat until combined, then gently stir in ricotta.

serves 4
per serving 32.4g fat; 3352kJ (802 cal)
tip You can use any kind of marinated vegetables (mushrooms, capsicum or mixed antipasti) in this recipe instead of the eggplant.

penne puttanesca

PREPARATION TIME 10 MINUTES   COOKING TIME 20 MINUTES

500g penne
$^1/_3$ cup (80ml) extra virgin olive oil
3 cloves garlic, crushed
1 teaspoon chilli flakes
5 medium tomatoes (950g),
    chopped coarsely
200g seeded kalamata olives
8 anchovy fillets, drained,
    chopped coarsely
$^1/_3$ cup (65g) rinsed drained capers
$^1/_3$ cup coarsely chopped fresh
    flat-leaf parsley
2 tablespoons finely shredded
    fresh basil

1   Cook pasta in large saucepan of boiling water, uncovered, until just tender.
2   Meanwhile, heat oil in large frying pan; cook garlic, stirring, until fragrant. Add chilli and tomato; cook, stirring, 5 minutes. Add remaining ingredients; cook, stirring occasionally, about 5 minutes or until sauce thickens slightly.
3   Add drained pasta to puttanesca sauce; toss gently to combine.

serves 4
per serving   21.2g fat; 2822kJ (674 cal)

prawn and sweet chilli salad

PREPARATION TIME 20 MINUTES COOKING TIME 5 MINUTES

You will need to buy about 1kg unpeeled prawns for this recipe. The dressing can be made two days ahead; assemble salad close to serving.

125g dried rice vermicelli
2 lebanese cucumbers (260g), seeded
2 medium carrots (240g)
150g bean sprouts
500g peeled cooked medium prawns
1/3 cup firmly packed coriander leaves
1/3 cup firmly packed vietnamese or round mint leaves

SWEET CHILLI DRESSING
1/3 cup (80ml) sweet chilli sauce
2 tablespoons fish sauce
1/3 cup (80ml) lime juice
3 small fresh red thai chillies, seeded, chopped finely

1 Place vermicelli in a large heatproof bowl; cover with boiling water. Stand until just tender; drain. Rinse under cold running water; drain well.
2 Meanwhile, cut cucumber and carrot thinly lengthways. Stack slices, slice again thinly lengthways to form long thin strips.
3 Combine vermicelli, cucumber, carrot, sprouts, prawns, herbs and sweet chilli dressing in large bowl; toss gently.
sweet chilli dressing Combine ingredients in screw-top jar; shake well.

serves 4
per serving 4g fat; 1270kJ (303·cal)
serving suggestion Serve topped with chopped roasted salted peanuts.

fettuccine with cauliflower and broccoli

PREPARATION TIME 10 MINUTES COOKING TIME 20 MINUTES

You need to buy half a medium cauliflower and about 450g of broccoli for this recipe.

125g butter

4 cloves garlic, crushed

¹/₂ cup (35g) stale breadcrumbs

2 anchovy fillets, chopped coarsely

4 cups (350g) coarsely chopped
   cauliflower

4 cups (350g) coarsely chopped
   broccoli

250g fettuccine

1   Heat butter in large frying pan; cook garlic and breadcrumbs, stirring, until breadcrumbs are golden brown. Stir in anchovy.

2   Bring large saucepan of water to a boil. Add cauliflower and broccoli; cook, stirring to ensure pieces separate. When vegetables are just tender, drain; rinse under cold water, drain.

3   Cook pasta in large saucepan of boiling water, uncovered, until just tender; drain.

4   Place pasta in large bowl with cauliflower, broccoli and breadcrumb mixture; toss gently to combine.

serves 4

per serving 26.1g fat; 2093kJ (501 cal)

spaghetti with rocket, parmesan and pine nuts

PREPARATION TIME 5 MINUTES COOKING TIME 10 MINUTES

200g spaghetti
¹/₄ cup (60ml) olive oil
2 cloves garlic, crushed
1 small fresh red thai chilli, chopped finely
¹/₄ cup (40g) roasted pine nuts
¹/₂ cup (40g) flaked parmesan cheese
100g baby rocket leaves

1 Cook pasta in large saucepan of boiling water, uncovered, until just tender; drain.

2 Meanwhile, heat oil in small saucepan; cook garlic and chilli, stirring, about 30 seconds or until garlic just softens and is fragrant (do not brown the garlic).

3 Place pasta and oil mixture in large bowl with pine nuts, cheese and rocket; toss to combine.

serves 4
per serving 24.6g fat; 1700kJ (407 cal)

angel hair frittata

PREPARATION TIME 10 MINUTES (PLUS STANDING TIME)
COOKING TIME 20 MINUTES

100g angel hair pasta
1 tablespoon vegetable oil
1 small leek (200g), chopped coarsely
2 cloves garlic, crushed
$^1/_4$ cup (20g) finely grated parmesan cheese
200g fetta cheese, crumbled
60g spinach leaves, chopped coarsely
$^1/_2$ cup (120g) sour cream
$^1/_4$ teaspoon ground nutmeg
6 eggs, beaten lightly

1 Cook pasta in large saucepan of boiling water, uncovered,
    until just tender; drain.
2 Meanwhile, heat oil in 20cm frying pan; cook leek and garlic,
    stirring, until leek softens.
3 Combine pasta and leek mixture in large bowl with cheeses,
    spinach, sour cream, nutmeg and egg. Pour mixture into same
    frying pan, cover; cook over low heat 10 minutes.
4 Remove cover; place under heated grill about 5 minutes or until frittata
    sets and top browns lightly. Stand in pan 5 minutes before serving.

serves 4
per serving 38.4g fat; 2202kJ (527 cal)
tip Angel hair pasta, the finest of pastas, produces the best results
in this frittata because it lends a smooth-textured consistency.

linguine with crab

PREPARATION TIME 10 MINUTES COOKING TIME 15 MINUTES

300g fresh crab meat
1 clove garlic, crushed
2 small fresh red thai chillies,
    seeded, sliced thinly
¹/₂ cup (125ml) dry white wine
1 tablespoon finely grated lemon rind
375g linguine
¹/₂ cup coarsely chopped fresh
    flat-leaf parsley
1 small red onion (100g), sliced thinly
¹/₃ cup (80ml) peanut oil

1 Cook crab, garlic and chilli in large heated non-stick frying pan, stirring, until crab is just cooked.
2 Add wine and rind; bring to a boil. Reduce heat; simmer, uncovered, until wine reduces by half.
3 Meanwhile, cook pasta in large saucepan of boiling water, uncovered, until just tender; drain.
4 Place pasta in large bowl with crab mixture and remaining ingredients; toss gently to combine.

serves 4
per serving 19.7g fat; 2299kJ (550 cal)

rigatoni with brie, walnut and mushroom sauce

PREPARATION TIME 5 MINUTES   COOKING TIME 20 MINUTES

1 tablespoon olive oil
1 clove garlic, crushed
200g button mushrooms, halved
1/2 cup (125ml) dry white wine
2 tablespoons wholegrain mustard
600ml light cream
375g rigatoni
200g brie cheese, chopped coarsely
1 cup (100g) walnuts, toasted,
  chopped coarsely
1/4 cup coarsely chopped fresh chives

1 Heat oil in large frying pan; cook garlic and mushroom, stirring, until mushroom is just tender. Add wine; boil, uncovered, until wine reduces by half.
2 Add mustard and cream to mushroom mixture; cook, stirring, until sauce thickens slightly.
3 Meanwhile, cook pasta in large saucepan of boiling water, uncovered, until just tender; drain.
4 Place pasta, cheese, walnuts, chives and sauce in large bowl; toss gently to combine.

serves 4
per serving 77.7g fat; 4686kJ (1121 cal)

spinach and ricotta dip

Boil, steam or microwave spinach leaves until just wilted; drain, chop finely. Blend or process spinach with chopped green onion, crushed garlic, lemon juice, olive oil, ricotta and fetta cheese until almost smooth. Serve with sliced ciabatta.

prosciutto with wild rocket

Arrange sliced prosciutto on individual serving plates. Gently toss wild rocket, parmesan cheese flakes, olive oil and lemon juice in medium bowl to combine; pile the rocket mixture on each serving plate with prosciutto.

sweet potato and spinach frittata

Combine chopped kumara and potato in large microwave-safe bowl, cover. Cook on HIGH (100%), stirring halfway through cooking, until just tender. Combine potato mixture with coarsely chopped baby spinach leaves, grated cheddar cheese and lightly beaten eggs; mix well. Spoon mixture into greased and lined cake pan. Bake in very hot oven until firm. Stand 5 minutes before serving.

vegetable kebabs with balsamic dressing

Thread chopped green capsicum, thickly sliced baby eggplant, cherry tomatoes, halved button mushrooms, thickly sliced zucchini and halved yellow patty-pan squash onto skewers. Cook the kebabs on heated oiled grill plate (or grill or barbecue) until browned all over. Combine olive oil and balsamic vinegar in screw-top jar, shake well; drizzle over kebabs.

asparagus and tomato salad

Combine steamed asparagus, cherry tomatoes, yellow teardrop tomatoes, rocket leaves, sliced avocado and shredded fresh basil; toss gently. Pour over combined olive oil, white vinegar, basil pesto and crushed garlic.

haloumi bruschetta

Cut a french bread stick into thick slices. Brush both sides with olive oil; toast slices until lightly browned. Top with char-grilled eggplant, sliced tomato and grilled haloumi. Serve bruschetta sprinkled with chopped parsley and drizzled with olive oil.

gnocchi with roasted pumpkin and burnt butter

Cut pumpkin into 1cm cubes, place on oiled oven tray. Roast, uncovered, in moderate oven 15 minutes or until just tender. Meanwhile, cook gnocchi in large saucepan of boiling water until just tender; drain. Melt butter and a little olive oil in same pan, add crushed garlic; cook, stirring until butter foams. Combine butter, pumpkin and gnocchi in large bowl; serve with parmesan flakes.

prawns and fetta in garlic tomato sauce

Heat oil in frying pan, add finely chopped onion and crushed garlic, cook until soft. Add dry white wine and undrained crushed canned tomatoes; bring to a boil, simmer until thickens. Add peeled and deveined, uncooked king prawns, chopped fresh parsley and oregano. Simmer, uncovered, until prawns are just cooked through. Serve sprinkled with crumbled fetta.

vegetarian

The quick-cooking methods used for most vegetarian meals, means that vegetables are the ideal food for cooks in a hurry. And with such a diversity available in the marketplace, you can have a different dish every night. Try pumpkin, basil and chilli stir-fry, green vegetable curry or a fast-cooking artichoke risotto.

ricotta gnocchi in fresh tomato sauce

PREPARATION TIME 10 MINUTES COOKING TIME 20 MINUTES

Gnocchi, the Italian word for dumplings, can be based on potato, flour, ricotta or polenta. Eggs and parmesan are usually added to the dough, which is then formed into little balls or shell shapes, cooked briefly in boiling water and served topped with butter, more parmesan or one of myriad savoury sauces.

500g firm ricotta cheese
1 cup (80g) finely grated parmesan cheese
$1/2$ cup (75g) plain flour
2 eggs, beaten lightly
1 tablespoon extra virgin olive oil
4 medium tomatoes (600g), chopped coarsely
6 green onions, sliced thinly
2 tablespoons coarsely chopped fresh oregano
2 tablespoons balsamic vinegar
2 tablespoons extra virgin olive oil, extra
$1/2$ cup (40g) shaved parmesan cheese

1 Bring large saucepan of water to a boil.
2 Meanwhile, combine ricotta, grated parmesan, flour, eggs and oil in large bowl. Drop rounded tablespoons of mixture into boiling water; cook, without stirring, until gnocchi float to the surface. Remove from pan with slotted spoon; drain, cover to keep warm.
3 Combine tomato, onion, oregano and vinegar in medium bowl.
4 Top warm gnocchi with fresh tomato sauce; drizzle with extra oil, top with shaved parmesan.

serves 4
per serving 40.6g fat; 2387kJ (570 cal)

mushroom, tomato and zucchini skewers with white bean puree

PREPARATION TIME 15 MINUTES COOKING TIME 15 MINUTES

1 large red onion (300g)
200g button mushrooms
250g cherry tomatoes
2 large zucchini (300g),
    chopped coarsely
2 tablespoons balsamic vinegar
2 tablespoons olive oil

WHITE BEAN PUREE
2 x 400g cans white beans,
    rinsed, drained
1 cup (250ml) chicken stock
1 clove garlic, quartered
1 tablespoon lemon juice
1 tablespoon olive oil

1 Cut onion through the middle into 12 wedges.
2 Thread onion, mushrooms, tomatoes and zucchini equally among 12 skewers. Place skewers on large tray; drizzle with combined vinegar and oil.
3 Cook skewers on heated oiled grill plate (or grill or barbecue) until browned all over and tender.
4 Serve skewers on white bean puree.
   white bean puree Combine beans and stock in large saucepan; bring to a boil. Reduce heat; simmer, uncovered, about 10 minutes or until liquid is absorbed. Blend or process bean mixture with garlic, juice and oil until smooth.

serves 4
per serving 14.7g fat; 882kJ (211 cal)

artichoke risotto

PREPARATION TIME 10 MINUTES COOKING TIME 25 MINUTES

A simple covered cooking method replaces the usual labour-intensive non-stop stirring required in more traditional risottos. Best results will be achieved by using arborio rice, but you can use any medium-grain rice, such as calrose.

2 teaspoons olive oil
1 medium brown onion (150g),
   chopped finely
3 cloves garlic, crushed
6 green onions, sliced thinly
2 cups (400g) medium-grain white rice
¾ cup (180ml) dry white wine
1½ cups (375ml) chicken stock
3 cups (750ml) water
400g can artichoke hearts, drained,
   sliced thinly
½ cup (40g) finely grated parmesan cheese

1 Heat oil in large saucepan; cook brown onion, garlic and half of the green onion, stirring, until brown onion softens. Add rice, wine, stock and the water; bring to a boil. Reduce heat; simmer, covered, 15 minutes, stirring occasionally.

2 Stir in artichokes, cheese and remaining green onion; cook, stirring, about 5 minutes or until artichokes are heated through.

serves 6
per serving 4.5g fat; 1353kJ (323 cal)
serving suggestion A salad of grape tomatoes, sliced fennel and a few fresh basil leaves suits this risotto perfectly.

cauliflower, pea and fried tofu curry

PREPARATION TIME 10 MINUTES   COOKING TIME 30 MINUTES

You will need a small cauliflower weighing approximately 1kg to make this recipe.

2 tablespoons olive oil
1 medium brown onion (150g), chopped coarsely
2 cloves garlic, crushed
900g cauliflower florets
1 teaspoon ground cumin
¹/₂ teaspoon ground coriander
¹/₂ teaspoon ground turmeric
¹/₄ teaspoon cayenne pepper
1 teaspoon garam marsala
410g can tomatoes
1 cup (250ml) vegetable stock
400g firm tofu
¹/₄ cup (60ml) vegetable oil
1 cup (120g) frozen peas, thawed

1 Heat olive oil in large saucepan, add onion and garlic; cook, stirring, until onion softens.
2 Add cauliflower and spices; cook, stirring, 2 minutes. Add undrained crushed tomatoes and stock, stir to combine; bring to a boil. Reduce heat; simmer, covered, 10 minutes or until cauliflower softens slightly.
3 Meanwhile, cut tofu into 1cm cubes. Heat vegetable oil in medium frying pan; cook tofu, in batches, until lightly coloured and crisp on all sides, drain on absorbent paper.
4 Add tofu and peas to cauliflower curry.

serves 4
per serving 26.5g fat; 1422kJ (340 cal)
tip This recipe is best made close to serving so tofu stays crisp.
serving suggestion Serve with boiled or steamed basmati rice.

stir-fried vegetables and tofu in black bean sauce

PREPARATION TIME 20 MINUTES COOKING TIME 10 MINUTES

450g hokkien noodles

300g fresh firm tofu

2 tablespoons peanut oil

1 medium eggplant (300g),
   cut into thin strips

1 medium carrot (120g), sliced thinly

1 medium red capsicum (200g),
   sliced thinly

230g can sliced water chestnuts,
   rinsed, drained

1 clove garlic, crushed

2cm piece fresh ginger (10g),
   grated finely

250g broccolini, chopped coarsely

500g choy sum, chopped coarsely

2 tablespoons kecap manis

$^{1}/_{2}$ cup (125ml) black bean sauce

1 Place noodles in large heatproof bowl; cover with boiling water. Use fork to separate noodles; drain.

2 Drain tofu, cut into 12 pieces. Heat half of the oil in wok or large frying pan; stir-fry tofu, in batches, until lightly browned. Drain on absorbent paper; cover to keep warm.

3 Heat half of the remaining oil in wok; stir-fry eggplant until soft. Add carrot, capsicum and water chestnuts; stir-fry until vegetables are just tender, remove from wok.

4 Heat remaining oil in wok; stir-fry garlic and ginger until fragrant. Add broccolini and choy sum; stir-fry until vegetables are just tender. Add noodles, sauces and eggplant mixture; stir-fry until heated through. Add tofu; toss gently to combine.

serves 6
per serving 14.3g fat; 1356kJ (324 cal)

rice with mushrooms and spinach

PREPARATION TIME 10 MINUTES COOKING TIME 25 MINUTES

3 cups (750ml) vegetable stock
¹/₄ cup (60ml) dry white wine
1 tablespoon finely grated lemon rind
1 medium brown onion (150g),
   chopped finely
2 cloves garlic, crushed
250g swiss brown mushrooms, halved
150g button mushrooms, halved
1¹/₂ cups (300g) medium-grain
   white rice
2 tablespoons lemon juice
1 cup (250ml) water
100g baby spinach leaves, torn
¹/₂ cup (40g) finely grated
   parmesan cheese
2 tablespoons shredded fresh
   basil leaves

1 Heat 1 tablespoon of the stock with wine and rind in large saucepan; cook onion and garlic, stirring, until onion softens. Add mushrooms; cook, stirring, 5 minutes.

2 Stir in rice, juice, the water and remaining stock. Bring to a boil, reduce heat; simmer, covered, about 20 minutes or until rice is tender.

3 Just before serving, stir in spinach, cheese and basil.

serves 4
per serving 4.9g fat; 1603kJ (383 cal)
tip Flat-leaf parsley can be substituted for the basil.
serving suggestion A balsamic-dressed mesclun salad and olive or sourdough bread turn this dish into a meal.

pumpkin, basil and chilli stir-fry

PREPARATION TIME 10 MINUTES COOKING TIME 15 MINUTES

1/3 cup (80ml) peanut oil
1 large brown onion (200g), sliced thinly
2 cloves garlic, sliced thinly
4 small fresh red thai chillies, sliced thinly
1kg pumpkin, chopped coarsely
250g sugar snap peas
1 teaspoon brown sugar
1/4 cup (60ml) vegetable stock
2 tablespoons soy sauce
3/4 cup loosely packed opal basil leaves
4 green onions, sliced thinly
1/2 cup (75g) roasted unsalted peanuts

1 Heat oil in wok or large frying pan; cook brown onion, in batches, until browned and crisp. Drain on absorbent paper.
2 Stir-fry garlic and chilli in wok until fragrant. Add pumpkin; stir-fry until browned all over and just tender. Add peas, sugar, stock and sauce; stir-fry until sauce thickens slightly.
3 Remove from heat; toss basil, green onion and nuts through stir-fry until well combined. Serve topped with fried onion.

serves 4
per serving 20.7g fat; 1436kJ (343 cal)
tip Remove the leaves from the stems of opal basil carefully without tearing or bruising.

green curry vegetables

PREPARATION TIME 20 MINUTES COOKING TIME 20 MINUTES

Broccolini is milder and sweeter than traditional broccoli, is completely edible from flower to stem, and has a delicate flavour with a subtle, peppery edge. It is a cross between broccoli and chinese kale (also known as chinese broccoli or gai larn).

100g snake beans
1 tablespoon peanut oil
1 medium brown onion (150g),
   sliced thinly
3 kaffir lime leaves, shredded finely
2 tablespoons green curry paste
1 medium carrot (120g), sliced thinly
2 baby eggplants (120g), sliced thickly
3¹/₄ cups (810ml) light coconut milk
350g butternut pumpkin, sliced thinly
4 medium yellow patty-pan squash
   (120g), quartered
100g button mushrooms, sliced thinly
250g broccolini, chopped coarsely
1 small red capsicum (150g),
   sliced thinly
230g can sliced bamboo
   shoots, drained

1 Cut beans into 5cm lengths.
2 Heat oil in large saucepan; cook onion and lime leaves, stirring, until onion softens. Stir in paste; cook, stirring, until fragrant. Add carrot and eggplant; cook, uncovered, until eggplant is just tender.
3 Add coconut milk; bring to a boil. Reduce heat; add pumpkin and squash. Simmer, uncovered, until squash is just tender. Add remaining ingredients; return to a boil. Reduce heat; simmer, stirring, about 5 minutes or until vegetables are tender.

serves 4
per serving 21.3g fat; 1293kJ (309 cal)
tips Commercially prepared green curry pastes can vary in strength from mild to mouth-searing, so you may need to adjust the amount used.
We used light coconut milk to reduce the fat count in this recipe; you can use regular coconut milk if you prefer.
serving suggestion Serve this curry with steamed jasmine rice.

corn and zucchini fritters with salsa

PREPARATION TIME 10 MINUTES COOKING TIME 10 MINUTES

If you're concerned about the fat count, use a non-stick frying pan sprayed with cooking-oil spray rather than shallow-frying the fritters.

50g butter, melted

¹/₂ cup (125ml) milk

³/₄ cup (110g) plain flour

2 eggs, beaten lightly

210g can creamed corn

2 medium zucchini (240g), grated coarsely

vegetable oil, for shallow-frying

SALSA

3 medium egg tomatoes (225g), chopped coarsely

2 medium avocados (500g), chopped coarsely

1 small red onion (100g), chopped coarsely

2 tablespoons lime juice

2 tablespoons finely chopped fresh coriander

1 Combine butter, milk, flour and egg in medium bowl; whisk until smooth. Add corn and zucchini; mix well.

2 Heat oil in medium frying pan; cook heaped tablespoons of batter, one at a time, about 2 minutes each side or until browned both sides and cooked through. Drain on absorbent paper. Serve with salsa.

salsa Combine ingredients in a small bowl.

serves 4

per serving 57.6g fat; 2922kJ (699 cal)

tip Keep cooked fritters warm in oven until serving time.

sides

This selection of delicious side dishes will transform your meal into a culinary triumph. Try an accompaniment of potato salad with herb vinaigrette, asparagus and pink grapefruit salad or wok-tossed greens with oyster sauce. These fast sides can be prepared at the same time as your main dish.

asparagus and pink grapefruit salad

PREPARATION TIME 20 MINUTES

It is important to purchase very young, fresh asparagus for the salad as it is served raw. The dressing can be made several days ahead. Assemble the salad just before serving.

200g thin asparagus, trimmed
1 baby cos lettuce
1 small radicchio lettuce
1 medium avocado (250g), sliced thinly
2 pink grapefruit (800g), peeled, segmented

TARRAGON HONEY DRESSING
2 tablespoons extra virgin olive oil
2 tablespoons tarragon vinegar
2 teaspoons honey

1 Cut asparagus spears in half, split the tips into halves and the base into quarters lengthways.
2 Arrange lettuce, avocado, grapefruit and asparagus on serving plates. Serve drizzled with tarragon honey dressing.
tarragon honey dressing Combine ingredients in screw-top jar; shake well.

serves 4
per serving 19.6g fat; 1029kJ (246 cal)

potato salad with herb vinaigrette

PREPARATION TIME 15 MINUTES COOKING TIME 15 MINUTES

2kg tiny new potatoes, halved
$^{1}/_{3}$ cup finely chopped fresh mint
$^{1}/_{3}$ cup finely chopped fresh
flat-leaf parsley
$^{1}/_{3}$ cup (80ml) red wine vinegar
$^{1}/_{4}$ cup (60ml) olive oil
2 tablespoons brown sugar

1 Boil, steam or microwave potato until tender. Drain; keep warm.
2 Combine remaining ingredients in large bowl.
3 Gently toss potato with vinaigrette mixture until combined.

serves 8
per serving 7.4g fat; 1002kJ (239 cal)
tip Make the vinaigrette a day ahead to allow the flavours to blend, and refrigerate, covered, overnight.

spiced lentils

PREPARATION TIME 5 MINUTES COOKING TIME 15 MINUTES

1½ cups (300g) red lentils
50g butter
1 small brown onion (80g), chopped finely
1 clove garlic, crushed
½ teaspoon ground coriander
½ teaspoon ground cumin
¼ teaspoon ground turmeric
¼ teaspoon cayenne pepper
½ cup (125ml) chicken stock
2 tablespoons coarsely chopped
   fresh flat-leaf parsley

1 Cook lentils, uncovered, in large saucepan of boiling water until just tender; drain.
2 Meanwhile, melt half of the butter in large frying pan; cook onion, garlic and spices, stirring, until onion softens.
3 Add lentils, stock and remaining butter; cook, stirring, until hot. Stir parsley into lentils off the heat.

serves 4
per serving 12.1g fat; 1248kJ (298 cal)

chats with black mustard seeds and sea salt

PREPARATION TIME 5 MINUTES   COOKING TIME 25 MINUTES

Tiny, waxy immature potatoes, harvested early in the season, are known as chats, baby potatoes or new potatoes.

1kg tiny new potatoes
2 tablespoons olive oil
1 tablespoon black mustard seeds
2 teaspoons sea salt flakes
1 teaspoon freshly ground black pepper
1 tablespoon coarsely chopped fresh flat-leaf parsley

1 Boil, steam or microwave potatoes until just tender; drain.
2 Heat oil in large frying pan; cook potatoes, stirring, until potatoes are browned lightly. Add mustard seeds, stirring, about 1 minute or until seeds pop.
3 Add remaining ingredients; toss gently to combine.

serves 4
per serving 9.5g fat; 1033kJ (247 cal)

cabbage and snow pea sprout salad

PREPARATION TIME 20 MINUTES

1 small savoy cabbage (1.2kg),
   shredded finely
1 medium yellow capsicum (200g),
   sliced thinly
160g snow pea sprouts
4 green onions, sliced thinly
$^{1}/_{3}$ cup (80ml) lemon juice
$^{1}/_{4}$ cup (60ml) peanut oil
$1^{1}/_{2}$ teaspoons sugar
1 tablespoon wholegrain mustard

1 Combine cabbage, capsicum, sprouts and onion in large
bowl; toss gently with combined remaining ingredients.

serves 8
per serving 7.3g fat; 377kJ (90 cal)
tips Use red cabbage for a spectacularly coloured salad.
Do not toss in the dressing until just before serving.

ginger-glazed baby carrots

PREPARATION 10 MINUTES COOKING TIME 5 MINUTES

800g baby carrots, peeled, trimmed
20g butter
1cm piece fresh ginger (5g),
   grated finely
2 teaspoons brown sugar
¹/₄ cup (60ml) fresh orange juice
1 tablespoon small fresh chervil leaves

1 Boil, steam or microwave carrots until just tender. Drain; remove from pan.
2 Add butter, ginger, sugar and juice to same pan; simmer, uncovered 1 minute.
3 Return carrots to pan; toss gently to combine.
4 Serve sprinkled with chervil.

serves 4
per serving 4.3g fat; 389kJ (93 cal)

stir-fried cauliflower, choy sum and snake beans

PREPARATION TIME 20 MINUTES   COOKING TIME 10 MINUTES

1 tablespoon peanut oil
2 cloves garlic, crushed
1 teaspoon ground turmeric
1 teaspoon finely chopped coriander root
4 green onions, sliced thinly
500g cauliflower florets
¼ cup (60ml) water
200g snake beans, cut into 5cm pieces
200g choy sum, chopped coarsely
1 tablespoon lime juice
1 tablespoon soy sauce
1 tablespoon coarsely chopped fresh coriander

1 Heat oil in wok or large frying pan; cook garlic, turmeric, coriander root and onion; stir-fry until onion just softens. Remove from wok; keep warm.

2 Stir-fry cauliflower with the water in wok until cauliflower is almost tender. Add beans and choy sum; stir-fry until vegetables are just tender.

3 Add juice, sauce, chopped coriander and onion mixture; stir-fry until heated through.

serves 4
per serving 5.4g fat; 385kJ (92 cal)

roasted tomato salad

PREPARATION TIME 20 MINUTES COOKING TIME 5 MINUTES

500g tear-drop tomatoes, halved
500g cherry tomatoes, halved
2 tablespoons olive oil
¹⁄₃ cup finely chopped fresh
   flat-leaf parsley
2 small fresh red thai chillies,
   seeded, sliced thinly, optional
2 tablespoons balsamic vinegar
¹⁄₃ cup (80ml) olive oil, extra

1 Preheat oven to hot.
2 Combine tomatoes, oil, parsley and chilli in large baking dish.
   Bake, uncovered, in hot oven about 5 minutes or until just soft.
3 Serve tomatoes, warm or cooled, drizzled with combined vinegar
   and extra oil.

serves 4
per serving 27.5g fat; 1149kJ (275 cal)

wok-tossed greens with oyster sauce

PREPARATION TIME 10 MINUTES   COOKING TIME 10 MINUTES

2 tablespoons peanut oil
4 cloves garlic, chopped finely
500g flat mushrooms, sliced thickly
1 tablespoon sesame seeds
400g baby bok choy, quartered
600g choy sum, chopped coarsely
4 green onions, chopped coarsely
2 tablespoons light soy sauce
$^1/_3$ cup (80ml) oyster sauce
1 teaspoon sesame oil

1   Heat half of the peanut oil in wok or large frying pan; stir-fry garlic, mushroom and seeds until mushroom just soften. Remove from wok.

2   Heat remaining peanut oil in wok; stir-fry bok choy and choy sum until just wilted. Return mushroom mixture to wok with onion, combined sauces and sesame oil; stir-fry until heated through.

serves 8
per serving   6.5g fat; 397kJ (95 cal)
tips   You can use any leafy asian vegetable you like in this recipe. Do not cook this recipe until just before serving.
serving suggestions   For some added spice, serve with a side bowl of sambal oelek.

tabbouleh

PREPARATION TIME 15 MINUTES (PLUS STANDING TIME)

Made with fresh parsley, mint and burghul (crushed processed wheat kernels), tabbouleh is a cornerstone of Middle-Eastern cuisine. You will need about three bunches of flat-leaf parsley for this recipe.

$^1/_2$ cup (80g) burghul
3 cups loosely packed, coarsely chopped fresh flat-leaf parsley
3 medium tomatoes (450g), chopped finely
1 small red onion (100g), chopped finely
1 cup coarsely chopped fresh mint
$^1/_2$ cup (125ml) lemon juice
$^1/_4$ cup (60ml) olive oil

1 Cover burghul with water in small bowl; stand about 10 minutes or until burghul softens. Drain in fine strainer; squeeze out excess liquid.
2 Meanwhile, combine parsley, tomato, onion and mint in large bowl; add burghul.
3 Toss salad gently with combined juice and oil.

serves 4
per serving 14.4g fat; 916kJ (219 cal)
tip Parsley can be chopped using scissors.

baby beet salad

PREPARATION TIME 20 MINUTES

850g can whole baby beets, rinsed,
  drained, quartered
1 cup bean sprouts (80g)
1 medium carrot (120g), sliced thinly
1 trimmed celery stalk (100g),
  sliced thinly
1 small red onion (100g), sliced thinly
$^{1}/_{2}$ cup loosely packed fresh mint leaves
1 tablespoon finely grated lime rind
$^{1}/_{4}$ cup (60ml) lime juice
2 tablespoons olive oil

1 Place beets, sprouts, carrot, celery, onion and mint in large serving bowl.
2 Combine remaining ingredients in screw-top jar; shake well.
3 Drizzle dressing over salad; toss gently to combine.

serves 4
per serving 9.4g fat; 707kJ (169 cal)

roasted vegetable and balsamic salad

PREPARATION TIME 10 MINUTES (PLUS STANDING TIME) COOKING TIME 25 MINUTES

¹/₄ cup (60ml) olive oil
1 clove garlic, crushed
2 large zucchini (300g)
4 medium flat mushrooms
    (500g), quartered
4 large egg tomatoes (360g), quartered
1 medium red onion (170g),
    cut into wedges
150g lamb's lettuce, trimmed
¹/₃ cup coarsely chopped basil

DRESSING
¹/₄ cup (60ml) olive oil
2 tablespoons balsamic vinegar
¹/₂ teaspoon sugar
¹/₂ teaspoon dijon mustard
1 clove garlic, crushed

1 Preheat oven to hot.
2 Combine oil and garlic in small bowl. Halve zucchini lengthways then
   chop into thin wedge-shaped pieces on the diagonal.
3 Arrange zucchini, mushroom, tomato and onion pieces, in single layer,
   on oven trays, brush with garlic-flavoured oil; roast, uncovered, in hot
   oven about 20 minutes or until browned lightly and just tender. Remove
   vegetables from oven; cool.
4 Combine cold vegetables in large bowl with lettuce and basil. Add dressing;
    toss to combine.
   dressing Combine ingredients in screw-top jar; shake well.

serves 4
per serving 28.2g fat; 1321kJ (316 cal)

white bean salad with coriander, mint and lemon grass

PREPARATION TIME 15 MINUTES

2 x 400g cans cannellini beans, rinsed, drained
150g baby spinach leaves
1 small red onion (100g), sliced thinly
1 clove garlic, crushed
1 tablespoon coarsely chopped fresh coriander
1 tablespoon coarsely chopped fresh mint
1 tablespoon thinly sliced fresh lemon grass
1cm piece fresh ginger (5g), grated finely
2 tablespoons sesame oil
2 tablespoons soy sauce
2 tablespoons sweet chilli sauce
2 tablespoons lime juice
1 teaspoon honey
2 small fresh red thai chillies, seeded, sliced thinly

1 Combine beans in large bowl with spinach and onion.
2 Combine garlic, herbs, lemon grass, ginger, oil, sauces, juice and honey in screw-top jar; shake well.
3 Drizzle dressing over salad; toss gently to combine, then sprinkle with chilli.

serves 4
per serving 9.8g fat; 558kJ (133 cal)

creamed spinach mash

PREPARATION TIME 15 MINUTES COOKING TIME 15 MINUTES

1kg potatoes, chopped coarsely
20g butter
1 clove garlic, crushed
125g baby spinach leaves
300ml cream, warmed

1 Boil, steam or microwave potato until tender; drain.
2 Meanwhile, melt butter in large frying pan; cook garlic and spinach, stirring, until garlic is fragrant and spinach wilted. Blend or process spinach mixture with half of the cream until mixture is pureed.
3 Place hot potato in large bowl; mash until smooth, then stir in spinach puree and remaining cream.

serves 4
per serving 37.2g fat; 2025kJ (484 cal)

moroccan-style carrot and orange salad

PREPARATION TIME 15 MINUTES

500g small carrots, peeled
2 small oranges (360g),
    peeled, segmented
$^1/_2$ small red onion (40g), sliced
$^1/_4$ cup fresh coriander leaves
1 tablespoon orange flower water
2 tablespoons caster sugar
2 tablespoons lemon juice

1 Cut carrots into thin strips. Combine carrots and remaining
   ingredients in large bowl.

serves 6
per serving 0.1g fat; 315kJ (75 cal)

stir-fried chinese broccoli

PREPARATION TIME 10 MINUTES   COOKING TIME 10 MINUTES

Chinese broccoli, also known as gai larn, has become a mainstay in a yum cha menu – and one of our favourite vegetables.

1kg chinese broccoli, trimmed, chopped coarsely
1 tablespoon peanut oil
5 green onions, chopped coarsely
2 cloves garlic, crushed
2cm piece fresh ginger (10g), grated finely
2 tablespoons soy sauce
2 tablespoons oyster sauce
1 tablespoon fish sauce
¼ cup (60ml) kecap manis
2 tablespoons sesame seeds

1 Boil, steam or microwave chinese broccoli until just tender; drain.
2 Heat oil in wok or large frying pan; stir-fry onion, garlic and ginger until fragrant. Add chinese broccoli, soy sauce, oyster sauce and fish sauce; stir until heated through. Drizzle with kecap manis; toss with sesame seeds.

serves 4
per serving 8.1g fat; 588kJ (140 cal)

spicy roasted pumpkin couscous

PREPARATION TIME 10 MINUTES COOKING TIME 20 MINUTES

1 tablespoon olive oil
2 cloves garlic, crushed
1 large red onion (300g), sliced thickly
500g pumpkin, peeled, chopped coarsely
3 teaspoons ground cumin
2 teaspoons ground coriander
1 cup (200g) couscous
1 cup (250ml) boiling water
20g butter
2 tablespoons coarsely chopped
  fresh flat-leaf parsley

1 Preheat oven to hot.

2 Heat oil in medium flameproof baking dish; cook garlic, onion and pumpkin, stirring, until vegetables are browned lightly. Add spices; cook, stirring, about 2 minutes or until fragrant.

3 Place baking dish in hot oven; roast pumpkin mixture, uncovered, about 15 minutes or until pumpkin is just tender.

4 Meanwhile, combine couscous with the water and butter in large heatproof bowl; cover, stand about 5 minutes or until water is absorbed, fluffing with fork occasionally.

5 Add pumpkin mixture to couscous; stir in parsley.

serves 4
per serving 9.8g fat; 1361kJ (325 cal)

snow pea stir-fry with sesame seeds and pine nuts

PREPARATION TIME 10 MINUTES   COOKING TIME 10 MINUTES

1 tablespoon sesame oil
600g snow peas, trimmed
2 green onions, sliced thinly
2 tablespoons toasted pine nuts
1 tablespoon toasted sesame seeds

1 Heat oil in wok or large frying pan; stir-fry snow peas and
    onion about 5 minutes or until snow peas are just tender.
2 Add nuts and seeds to wok; stir-fry briefly to combine.

serves 4
per serving   11.5g fat; 657kJ (157 cal)

shaved fennel and parmesan salad

PREPARATION TIME 15 MINUTES

6 baby fennel (780g), trimmed
100g piece parmesan cheese
¼ cup loosely packed fennel tops

LEMON VINAIGRETTE
¼ cup (60ml) extra virgin olive oil
2 tablespoons lemon juice
2 teaspoons finely chopped fennel tops
1 clove garlic, crushed
1 teaspoon dijon mustard
1 teaspoon sugar

1 Using a mandolin, V-slicer or sharp knife, slice fennel thinly. Using a vegetable peeler, peel flakes from cheese.
2 Just before serving, combine fennel, cheese and fennel tops in large bowl. Add lemon vinaigrette, toss gently.
   lemon vinaigrette Combine ingredients in screw-top jar; shake well.

serves 6
per serving 14.6g fat; 736kJ (176 cal)
tip The lemon vinaigrette can be made a day ahead. Assemble the salad close to serving.

cheesy pesto polenta

PREPARATION TIME 10 MINUTES   COOKING TIME 25 MINUTES

2^1/$_3$ cups (580ml) water
2^1/$_3$ cups (580ml) milk
1 cup (170g) polenta
^{1}/$_2$ cup (40g) finely grated
   parmesan cheese
30g butter, chopped

PESTO
2 tablespoons finely grated
   parmesan cheese
2 tablespoons toasted pine nuts
2 tablespoons olive oil
1 clove garlic, crushed
1 cup firmly packed fresh basil leaves

1 Combine the water and milk in large saucepan; bring to a boil.
   Gradually sprinkle polenta over milk mixture; cook, stirring, until
   polenta thickens slightly.
2 Reduce heat; simmer, uncovered, about 20 minutes or until polenta
   is thickened, stirring occasionally. Stir in cheese, butter and pesto.
   pesto Blend or process ingredients until mixture forms a paste.

serves 4
per serving 31.3g fat; 2023kJ (483 cal)

zucchini with chorizo

PREPARATION TIME 10 MINUTES COOKING TIME 10 MINUTES

1 fresh chorizo sausage (170g)
4 medium zucchini (480g), sliced

1 Squeeze filling from the sausage casing; add to large heated frying pan and cook, stirring, until sausage browns and crumbles. Remove from pan, leaving fat in pan.
2 Add zucchini to same pan and cook, stirring, until zucchini is browned and tender.
3 Return sausage to pan, cook, stirring, until combined. Serve immediately.

serves 8
Per serving 7.7 fat; 385kJ (92 cal)
tip If fresh chorizo is unavailable, substitute sliced semi-dried chorizo (salami-style).

beef in asian broth

Combine water, canned beef consommé, grated fresh ginger and soy sauce in saucepan; bring to a boil. Add bean thread noodles; simmer until just tender. Add thinly sliced beef rump steak, sliced red capsicum, fresh baby corn, chopped baby bok choy and bean sprouts; stir until soup is heated through.

clear prawn soup

Combine chicken stock with grated fresh ginger, chopped fresh lemon grass, lemon juice, fish sauce and sambal oelek. Bring to a boil; simmer 5 minutes. Add prawns, reduce heat; simmer until prawns just change colour. Ladle soup into bowls, serve sprinkled with coriander leaves.

moroccan chickpea soup

Heat oil in saucepan, add chopped onion, crushed garlic and grated ginger; cook until soft. Add moroccan seasoning; cook until fragrant. Add chicken stock, undrained crushed canned tomatoes, rinsed and drained canned chickpeas. Bring to a boil; simmer 10 minutes. Serve sprinkled with chopped fresh coriander.

chicken laksa

Heat oil in saucepan, cook laksa paste until fragrant. Stir in light coconut milk, chicken stock, lime juice, fish sauce, a pinch of sugar and torn kaffir lime leaves; bring to a boil. Add chopped cooked chicken, stir until heated through. Place rinsed and drained fresh egg noodles in serving bowls, ladle laksa over noodles; top with bean sprouts and mint leaves.

soups

chicken and corn soup

Heat peanut oil in saucepan, add coarsely chopped green onion and crushed garlic; cook until soft. Add chicken stock. Bring to a boil, add finely chopped chicken breast fillets; simmer until chicken is cooked. Add canned creamed corn and canned corn kernels; simmer until heated through.

Thai-style pumpkin soup

Cook red curry paste, stirring, in saucepan until fragrant. Add canned cream of pumpkin soup, light coconut milk and chicken stock; bring to a boil. Add coarsely chopped cooked chicken; stir until chicken heated through. Stir in sliced green onion and thinly sliced fresh basil.

minestrone on the run

Heat oil in saucepan, add onion and crushed garlic; cook, stirring, until soft. Add chopped carrot, celery and parsnip; cook, stirring, 5 minutes. Add undrained crushed canned tomatoes, tomato paste and chicken stock. Bring to a boil; add macaroni and rinsed and drained canned borlotti beans. Simmer until macaroni is cooked. Serve sprinkled with parmesan cheese.

pea and potato soup

Melt butter in saucepan; cook sliced leek and celery until soft. Add peeled and chopped potato and chicken stock; cover, bring to a boil, simmer until potato softens. Add frozen peas; cook 5 minutes or until peas are soft. Blend or process soup, in batches, until smooth. Serve drizzled with cream.

dessert

A tasty way to end your meal is with one of these scrumptious desserts. They are all fast to make, and will disappear just as quickly. White chocolate fondue, melon and pineapple with honey lime syrup, or summer berry sundae are just some of the treats in store.

warm pavlovas with berry compote

PREPARATION TIME 15 MINUTES COOKING TIME 25 MINUTES

Berry compote can be made a day ahead and served cold or reheated to serve warm with pavlovas. Pavlovas must be made close to serving as they will deflate.

3 egg whites
2 cups (320g) icing sugar mixture
½ cup (125ml) boiling water
300ml cream, whipped

BERRY COMPOTE
½ cup (125ml) raspberry cranberry fruit drink
1 tablespoon lemon juice
¼ cup (55g) caster sugar
1 tablespoon cornflour
1 tablespoon water
500g frozen mixed berries

1 Place oven rack on lowest shelf. Preheat oven to moderate. Line large oven tray with baking paper.
2 Beat egg whites, icing sugar and water in small bowl with an electric mixer about 8 minutes or until firm peaks form.
3 Using a large metal spoon, drop six equal portions of mixture onto prepared tray. Bake on lowest shelf, in moderate oven, about 25 minutes or until browned lightly and firm to touch.
4 Serve pavlovas immediately topped with warm berry compote and cream.
berry compote Combine fruit drink, lemon juice and sugar in a medium saucepan; stir over heat, without boiling, until sugar is dissolved. Add blended cornflour and water to saucepan; stir over heat until mixture boils and thickens. Stir in berries.

serves 6
per serving 9.8g fat; 1560kJ (373 cal)

pear and plum amaretti crumble

PREPARATION TIME 10 MINUTES   COOKING TIME 15 MINUTES

825g can plums in syrup, drained,
  halved, stoned
825g can pear halves in natural juice,
  drained, halved
1 teaspoon ground cardamom
125g amaretti (almond macaroons),
  crushed
¹/₃ cup (50g) plain flour
¹/₃ cup (40g) ground almonds
¹/₂ cup (70g) slivered almonds
100g butter, chopped

1 Preheat oven to moderately hot. Grease deep 6-cup (1.5-litre)
   ovenproof dish.
2 Place plums, pears and cardamom in prepared dish; toss
   gently to combine.
3 Combine amaretti, flour, ground almonds and nuts in medium
   bowl. Using fingers, rub butter into amaretti mixture, sprinkle
   evenly over plum mixture.
4 Bake, uncovered, in moderately hot oven about 15 minutes or
   until golden brown.

serves 4
per serving 39.8g fat; 2852kJ (681 cal)
tip Crumbles also may be made in four 1½-cup (375ml)
individual dishes and baked for 15 minutes.

oranges in cinnamon syrup

PREPARATION TIME 10 MINUTES (PLUS STANDING TIME) COOKING TIME 10 MINUTES

¾ **cup (165g) caster sugar**
¼ **cup (60ml) rum**
½ **cup (125ml) water**
1 strip orange peel
1 cinnamon stick
2 whole cloves
2 cardamom pods, bruised
4 large oranges (1.2kg), peeled

1 Combine sugar, rum and water in medium saucepan; stir over medium heat, without boiling, until sugar is dissolved. Add peel and spices, bring to the boil then simmer, uncovered, about 5 minutes or until thickened slightly.

2 Remove from heat; add oranges to pan, stand 5 minutes.

3 Serve oranges and a little syrup with ice-cream, if desired.

serves 4
per serving 0.2g fat; 1127kJ (269 cal)

caramelised apple tart

PREPARATION TIME 10 MINUTES COOKING TIME 20 MINUTES

4 small apples (520g)
50g butter
$^1/_4$ cup (55g) firmly packed brown sugar
$^1/_2$ teaspoon ground cinnamon
$^1/_2$ cup (50g) pecans
$^1/_4$ cup (75g) apple sauce
2 teaspoons lemon juice
2 sheets ready-rolled butter puff pastry
1 egg, beaten lightly

1 Peel and core apples; slice thinly. Stir butter, sugar and cinnamon in medium saucepan over low heat until sugar dissolves; add apple. Cook, stirring occasionally, over low heat, until apple softens. Drain apple mixture over medium bowl; reserve caramel mixture.

2 Meanwhile, blend or process nuts, apple sauce and juice until mixture is smooth.

3 Preheat oven to moderately hot. Line oven tray with baking paper.

4 Cut eight 11cm rounds from pastry sheets; place four of the rounds on prepared tray; brush with egg. Using 9cm cutter, remove centres from four remaining rounds; centre pastry rings on top of the 11cm rounds.

5 Spread nut mixture in centre of rounds; arrange apple mixture on top. Bake tarts, uncovered, in moderately hot oven about 15 minutes or until golden brown. Serve warm, with heated reserved caramel mixture.

serves 4
per serving 39.7g fat; 2606kJ (623 cal)
tip We used Granny Smith apples in this recipe because their firm white flesh retains its shape and readily absorbs the butter and sugar mixture.

summer berry sundae

PREPARATION TIME 5 MINUTES COOKING TIME 15 MINUTES

*We used a combination of fresh blueberries, raspberries and strawberries
in the recipe. Berry mixture can be made a day ahead.*

¼ **cup (55g) caster sugar**
500g mixed fresh berries
1 tablespoon Cointreau or orange juice
1 litre vanilla ice-cream
²/₃ **cup (100g) macadamias,**
   chopped, toasted

1 Combine sugar and berries in medium saucepan and stir over low heat, without boiling, until the sugar is dissolved.

2 Bring to a boil and simmer, uncovered, about 5 minutes or until berries are soft. Stir in the liqueur and cool, if desired.

3 To serve, layer scoops of the ice-cream, berry mixture and nuts in four tall serving glasses.

serves 4
per serving 33g fat; 2206kJ (527 cal)
tip Toasting nuts enhances their flavour, texture and aroma.
Place the macadamias on an oven tray and bake, uncovered,
in a moderate oven, for 5 to 8 minutes or until browned lightly.

white chocolate fondue

PREPARATION TIME 10 MINUTES COOKING TIME 5 MINUTES

Traditionally, fondue is served in a single pot that sits in the middle of the table. Provide your guests with skewers, then watch them dip piece after piece of fruit or almond bread into the chocolate pot – this will prove a very popular way to finish the meal!

180g white cooking chocolate, chopped coarsely

¹/₂ cup (125ml) cream

1 tablespoon Malibu

1 cup (130g) strawberries

1 large banana (230g), chopped coarsely

150g fresh pineapple, chopped coarsely

8 slices (35g) almond bread

16 marshmallows (100g)

1 Combine chocolate and cream in small saucepan, stir over low heat until smooth; stir in liqueur. Transfer fondue to serving bowl.

2 Place fondue in centre of dining table; serve remaining ingredients on a platter.

serves 4

per serving 14.9g fat; 1100kJ (263 cal)

tip Fondue can be served with any of your favourite fruits.

soft-centred chocolate cakes with warm sour cherry sauce

PREPARATION TIME 15 MINUTES COOKING TIME 25 MINUTES

Sour cherry jam is made from morello cherries, which have a dark mahogany-red skin and flesh. The chocolate marries so well with the jam that this dessert is sure to please.

185g dark eating chocolate, chopped coarsely
185g butter, chopped
3 egg yolks
¹/₃ cup (50g) plain flour
4 eggs
¹/₃ cup (75g) caster sugar
350g jar sour cherry jam

1 Preheat oven to moderate. Grease Texas-style six-hole ¾-cup (180ml) muffin pan. Sprinkle with a little plain flour; tilt to coat side of holes, shake off excess.

2 Place chocolate and butter in small saucepan; stir over low heat until mixture is smooth. Transfer to large bowl; stir in yolks and flour.

3 Beat eggs and sugar in small bowl with electric mixer about 5 minutes or until light and fluffy. Fold egg mixture into chocolate mixture; spoon mixture into prepared pan. Bake in moderate oven about 10 minutes; cakes should be soft in the centre. Stand 5 minutes; remove cakes carefully from pan.

4 Meanwhile, melt jam in small saucepan over low heat; blend or process until smooth, strain. Return jam to saucepan, add a little water to give pouring consistency; bring to a boil. Skim surface; stand 5 minutes.

5 Serve warm soft-centred chocolate cakes drizzled with warm sour cherry sauce.

serves 6
per serving 40.1g fat; 2456kJ (587 cal)
tip Sour cherry jam can be found in most supermarkets.
serving suggestions Serve cakes topped with crème fraîche or whipped cream.

fresh pineapple with coconut

PREPARATION TIME 15 MINUTES

You will need about four passionfruit for this recipe. Recipe can be made several hours ahead. Sprinkle with coconut just before serving.

1 small pineapple (800g)
¹⁄₃ cup (80ml) passionfruit pulp
2 tablespoons Malibu
¼ cup (10g) flaked coconut, toasted

1 Peel, core and thinly slice pineapple.
2 Divide pineapple among serving dishes; drizzle with passionfruit and Malibu, sprinkle with coconut.

serves 4
per serving   1.8g fat; 433kJ (104 cal)
tip You can use an orange-flavoured liqueur in place of the rum, if preferred.

waffles and ice-cream à la suzette

PREPARATION TIME 10 MINUTES COOKING TIME 10 MINUTES

125g butter
$\frac{1}{2}$ cup (110g) caster sugar
2 teaspoons finely grated orange rind
1 tablespoon orange juice
$\frac{1}{4}$ cup (60ml) Cointreau
8 Belgian-style waffles
200ml vanilla ice-cream

1 Melt butter in small heavy-based saucepan; add sugar, rind, juice and liqueur. Stir over low heat, without boiling, until sugar dissolves; bring to a boil. Reduce heat; simmer, uncovered, without stirring, about 1 minute or until sauce thickens slightly.

2 Warm waffles according to manufacturer's instructions. Divide half of the waffles among serving plates; top with ice-cream, remaining waffles and suzette sauce.

serves 4
per serving 41.6g fat; 3012kJ (719 cal)

caramelised pear bruschetta

PREPARATION TIME 10 MINUTES COOKING TIME 10 MINUTES

$^1/_3$ cup (80ml) thickened cream
1 cup (200g) ricotta cheese
$^1/_4$ cup (50g) finely chopped crystallised ginger
1 tablespoon icing sugar mixture
6 corella pears (900g)
60g butter
$^1/_3$ cup (75g) firmly packed brown sugar
$^1/_4$ cup (60ml) orange juice
2 small brioche (200g)

1 Beat cream in small bowl with electric mixer until soft peaks form;
   fold in ricotta, ginger and icing sugar.
2 Cut each pear into eight wedges; remove and discard core and peel.
   Melt half of the butter in large frying pan; cook pear, stirring occasionally,
   until pear is browned lightly. Add remaining butter and brown sugar;
   cook, stirring, until pear just starts to caramelise. Add juice; cook,
   stirring, 1 minute.
3 Meanwhile, cut each brioche into four equal slices; toast until browned
   lightly both sides.
4 Divide brioche slices among serving plates; top with ricotta mixture then
   caramelised pear.

serves 4
per serving 31.5g fat; 2690kJ (644 cal)

chocolate rum mini mousse

PREPARATION TIME 10 MINUTES COOKING TIME 5 MINUTES

A variation on the Italian zabaglione, the rum and chocolate transform this into a dessert of great depth and contrasting flavours. Use a caribbean rum for this recipe, for its mild, smooth taste.

6 egg yolks
⅓ cup (75g) caster sugar
½ cup (125ml) dark rum, warmed
50g dark eating chocolate,
   grated finely

1 Beat egg yolks and sugar in small deep-sided heatproof bowl with electric mixer until light and fluffy.

2 Place bowl over small saucepan of simmering water; whisk egg mixture constantly while gradually adding rum. Continue to whisk until mixture is thick and creamy. Add chocolate, in two batches, whisking gently until chocolate melts between additions.

3 Pour mousse mixture into four ⅓-cup (80ml) serving glasses.

serves 4
per serving 12g fat; 1230kJ (294 cal)
tip The mousse can be served chilled if desired; refrigerate about 2 hours.
serving suggestion Serve with almond biscotti or almond bread.

peach galette

PREPARATION TIME 15 MINUTES COOKING TIME 20 MINUTES

2 medium peaches (300g)
6 sheets fillo pastry
60g butter, melted
3 teaspoons sugar
1 tablespoon apricot jam,
    warmed, sieved

1 Preheat oven to moderately hot. Line oven tray with baking paper.
2 Halve peaches, discard seeds; slice peach halves thinly.
3 Place two pastry sheets on board; brush lightly with a third of the butter. Top with two more pastry sheets; brush lightly with half of the remaining butter. Repeat layering with remaining pastry and butter.
4 Fold pastry in half to form a square; cut 22cm-diameter circle from pastry square. Arrange peach slices on pastry circle; sprinkle with sugar. Bake in moderately hot oven about 20 minutes or until galette browns.
5 Serve warm galette brushed with jam.

serves 4
per serving 12.8g fat; 911kJ (218 cal)
tips Cover the pastry with greaseproof paper or plastic wrap then a damp towel when you're working with it, to prevent it drying out. Nectarines, apricots, apples, plums and pears are all suitable to use in place of the peaches.

chocolate hazelnut self-saucing puddings

PREPARATION TIME 15 MINUTES   COOKING TIME 25 MINUTES

Nutella is a commercial spread made of milk chocolate and hazelnuts; it can be used in cooking, as here, or spread on your breakfast toast.

$^1/_2$ cup (125ml) milk
40g dark eating chocolate, chopped coarsely
50g butter
$^1/_3$ cup (35g) cocoa powder
$^1/_2$ cup (75g) self-raising flour
$^1/_4$ cup (25g) ground hazelnut
$^1/_3$ cup (75g) caster sugar
$^2/_3$ cup (150g) firmly packed brown sugar
1 egg, beaten lightly
$^3/_4$ cup (180ml) water
40g butter, chopped, extra
200ml vanilla ice-cream

CHOCOLATE HAZELNUT SAUCE
$^1/_2$ cup (125ml) cream
2 tablespoons brown sugar
50g dark eating chocolate, chopped finely
$^1/_3$ cup (110g) Nutella
1 tablespoon Frangelico

1 Preheat oven to moderate. Grease four 1-cup (250ml) ovenproof dishes.
2 Stir milk, chocolate, butter and half of the cocoa in small saucepan over low heat until smooth.
3 Combine flour, ground hazelnuts, caster sugar and half of the brown sugar in medium bowl. Add chocolate mixture and egg; stir until combined. Divide mixture among prepared dishes.
4 Stir the water, extra butter, remaining brown sugar and remaining cocoa in small saucepan over low heat until smooth. Pour hot mixture gently and evenly over puddings.
5 Bake puddings, uncovered, in moderate oven about 25 minutes. Stand 5 minutes; top with ice-cream then chocolate hazelnut sauce.
chocolate hazelnut sauce Combine cream and sugar in small saucepan. Bring to a boil; remove from heat. Add chocolate; stir until smooth. Add Nutella and liqueur; stir until smooth.

serves 4
per serving 58.6g fat; 4395kJ (1050 cal)
tip This dessert is best served hot because the sauce is quickly absorbed by the puddings.

melon and pineapple with honey lime syrup

PREPARATION TIME 10 MINUTES COOKING TIME 5 MINUTES

¹/₃ **cup (120g) honey**
¹/₂ **cup (125ml) lime juice**
400g fresh pineapple pieces
400g fresh honeydew melon pieces
200g honey-flavoured yogurt

1 Combine honey and juice in small saucepan; bring to a boil then simmer, uncovered, 5 minutes.

2 Pour honey mixture over fruit in large bowl and mix gently.

3 Serve fruit mixture with yogurt.

serves 4
per serving 1.4g fat; 717kJ (171 cal)

passionfruit soufflés

PREPARATION TIME 10 MINUTES   COOKING TIME 15 MINUTES

You need four large passionfruit for this recipe.

1 tablespoon caster sugar
2 egg yolks
¹/₃ cup (80ml) fresh passionfruit pulp
2 tablespoons Cointreau
¹/₂ cup (80g) icing sugar mixture
4 egg whites
2 teaspoons icing sugar mixture, extra

1 Preheat oven to moderate. Lightly grease four 1-cup (250ml) ovenproof dishes. Sprinkle insides of dishes evenly with caster sugar; shake away excess. Place dishes on oven tray.

2 Whisk yolks, passionfruit pulp, liqueur and 2 tablespoons of the icing sugar in large bowl until mixture is combined.

3 Beat egg whites in small bowl with electric mixer until soft peaks form. Gradually add remaining icing sugar; beat until firm peaks form.

4 Gently fold egg white mixture, in two batches, into passionfruit mixture; divide mixture among prepared dishes.

5 Bake, uncovered, in moderate oven about 12 minutes or until soufflés are puffed and browned lightly. Dust tops with extra sifted icing sugar. Serve immediately.

serves 4
per serving   2.5g fat; 749kJ (179 cal)
serving suggestion   Top with fresh passionfruit pulp and serve with cream or ice-cream.

ice-cream sundae with berry sauce and almond wafers

PREPARATION TIME 20 MINUTES   COOKING TIME 10 MINUTES

1/3 cup (75g) firmly packed brown sugar
25g butter
1/2 cup (125ml) thickened cream
1 cup (150g) frozen mixed berries
500ml vanilla ice-cream
500ml strawberry ice-cream

ALMOND WAFERS
1 egg white
2 tablespoons caster sugar
2 tablespoons plain flour
20g butter, melted
2 tablespoons flaked almonds

1 Make almond wafers.
2 Combine sugar, butter and cream in small saucepan; bring to a boil. Reduce heat; simmer, uncovered, stirring, about 5 minutes or until slightly thickened. Remove from heat; stir in berries.
3 Divide both ice-creams among four 1½-cup (375ml) serving glasses; drizzle with berry sauce. Serve with almond wafers.
almond wafers Preheat oven to moderate. Lightly grease two oven trays. Beat egg white in small bowl with electric mixer until soft peaks form. Gradually add sugar, beating until dissolved after each addition; fold in flour and butter.
Drop rounded teaspoons of mixture 10cm apart on greased oven trays (approximately four per tray); sprinkle with nuts. Bake, uncovered, in moderate oven about 5 minutes or until wafers are browned lightly; cool on trays.

serves 4
per serving 37.2g fat; 2447kJ (585 cal)

glossary

almonds flat, pointy-ended nuts with pitted brown shell enclosing a creamy white kernel that is covered by a brown skin.
flaked: paper-thin slices.
meal: also known as ground.
slivered: small lengthways-cut pieces.

angel hair pasta also known as barbina.

artichoke hearts tender centre of the globe artichoke; purchased in brine, canned or in glass jars.

baby beets, whole canned canned baby beetroot also known as red beets.

bacon rashers also known as bacon slices; made from cured and smoked pork.

bamboo shoots the tender shoots of bamboo plants, available in cans; must be drained and rinsed before use.

barbecue sauce a spicy, tomato-based sauce used to marinade, baste or as an accompaniment.

basil an aromatic herb; there are many types, but the most commonly used is sweet basil
thai: also known as horapa, is different from holy basil and sweet basil in both look and taste. Having smaller leaves and purplish stems, it has a slight licorice or aniseed taste, and is one of the basic flavours that typify Thai cuisine.
opal: large purple leaves and a sweet, almost gingery flavour. It has better keeping properties than most other basils, and can be used instead of thai, but not holy basil, in recipes.

bean sprouts also known as bean shoots; tender new growths of assorted beans and seeds germinated for consumption as sprouts. The most readily available are mung bean, soy bean, alfalfa and snow pea sprouts.

beetroot also known as red beets.

black bean sauce a chinese sauce made from fermented soy beans, spices, water and wheat flour, and is much used in stir-fry cooking.

black beans, salted soy beans that have been salted and fermented.

baby bok choy

bok choy

bok choy also known as bak choy, pak choi, chinese white cabbage or chinese chard, has a fresh, mild mustard taste; use stems and leaves, stir-fried or braised. Baby bok choy, also known as pak kat farang, shanghai bok choy, chinese chard or white cabbage, is small and more tender than bok choy. Its mildly acrid, distinctively appealing taste has brought baby bok choy to the forefront of commonly used asian greens.

breadcrumbs, stale one- or two-day-old bread that is made into crumbs by grating, blending or processing.

brioche rich, yeast-risen french bread made with butter and eggs. Available from pâtisseries or better bakeries.

broccolini a cross between broccoli and chinese kale, is milder and sweeter than broccoli. Each long stem is topped by a loose floret that closely resembles broccoli; from floret to stem, broccolini is completely edible.

burghul also known as bulghur wheat; hulled steamed wheat kernels that, once dried, are crushed into various size grains.

butter use salted or unsalted (sweet) butter; 125g is equal to 1 stick butter.

cannellini beans small, dried white bean similar in appearance and flavour to great northern and navy or haricot beans.

capsicum also known as bell pepper or, simply, pepper; they can be red, green, yellow, orange or purplish black. Seeds and membranes should be discarded before use.

cardamom a spice native to India, and used extensively in its cuisine; can be purchased in pod, seed or ground form. Has a distinctive aromatic, sweetly rich flavour.

cayenne pepper a thin-fleshed, long, extremely hot, dried red chilli, usually purchased ground; both arbol and guajillo chillies are the fresh sources for cayenne.

cheese
brie: smooth and voluptuous, brie has a bloomy white rind and a creamy centre that becomes runnier as it ripens.
fetta: Greek in origin; a crumbly textured goat- or sheep-milk cheese with a sharp, salty taste.
haloumi: a firm, cream-coloured sheep-milk cheese that is matured in brine; somewhat like a minty, salty fetta in flavour, haloumi can be grilled or fried, briefly, without crumbling and breaking down.

parmesan: also known as parmigiano, parmesan is a hard, grainy cow-milk cheese that originated in the Parma region of Italy. The curd is salted in brine for a month before being aged for up to two years in humid conditions. Parmesan is mainly grated as a topping for pasta, soups and other savoury dishes, but it is also delicious eaten with fruit.
ricotta: the name for this soft, white, cow-milk cheese roughly translates as cooked again. It's made from whey, a by-product of other cheese making, to which fresh milk and acid are added. Ricotta is a sweet, moist cheese with a fat content of around 8.5%, and a slightly grainy texture.

chickpeas also known as hummus, garbanzos or channa; an irregularly round, sandy-coloured legume.

chilli available in many different types and sizes; generally the smaller the chilli, the hotter it is. Removing seeds and membranes lessens the heat level.
flakes: deep-red, dehydrated chilli slices and whole seeds.
powder: the Asian variety, made from dried ground thai chillies, is the hottest; it can be used as a substitute for fresh chillies in the proportion of ½ teaspoon ground chilli powder to 1 medium chopped fresh chilli.
thai chillies: small, hot and bright red in colour.

chinese broccoli also known as gai lam, kanah, gai lum and chinese kale; appreciated more for its stems than its coarse leaves. Can be served steamed and stir-fried, in soups and noodle dishes.

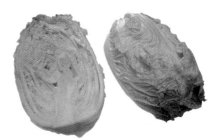

chinese cabbage also known as peking or napa cabbage, wong bok and petsai. Elongated in shape with pale green, crinkly leaves, this is the most common cabbage in South-East Asia. Can be shredded or chopped, and eaten raw or braised, steamed or stir-fried.

chocolate
dark eating: made of cocoa liquor, cocoa butter and sugar.
white: we used a cooking-quality chocolate.

chorizo sausage a sausage of Spanish origin, made of coarsely ground pork and highly seasoned with garlic and chillies.

choy sum also known as pakaukeo or flowering cabbage, a member of the bok choy family; easy to identify with its long stems, light green leaves and yellow flowers. Is eaten, stems and all, steamed or stir-fried.

cinnamon dried inner bark of the shoots of the cinnamon tree; available in stick or ground form.

cloves dried flower buds of a tropical tree; can be used whole or in ground form. Has a distinctively pungent and "spicy" scent and flavour, so should be used minimally.

cocoa powder also known as cocoa; dried, unsweetened, roasted then ground cocoa beans.

coconut
cream: obtained commercially from the first pressing of the coconut flesh, without the addition of water.
milk: the second pressing of the coconut flesh (less rich) is sold as coconut milk.
desiccated: unsweetened, concentrated, dried, finely-shredded coconut.
flaked: dried, flaked, coconut flesh.

Cointreau citrus-flavoured liqueur.

corella pears miniature dessert pears.

coriander also known as pak chee, cilantro or chinese parsley; bright-green-leafed herb with a pungent flavour. Both stems and roots of coriander are used in Thai cuisine; wash well before chopping.

cornflour also known as cornstarch; used as a thickening agent in cooking.

couscous a fine, grain-like cereal product, made from semolina.

curly endive also known as frisee, a curly-leafed green vegetable, mainly used in salads.

currants dried, tiny, almost black raisins so-named after a grape variety that originated in Corinth, Greece.

curry powder a blend of ground spices used for convenience when making Indian food. May consist of dried chilli, cinnamon, coriander, cumin, fennel, fenugreek, mace, cardamom and turmeric. Choose mild or hot to suit your taste and the recipe.

egg some recipes in this book may call for raw or barely cooked eggs; exercise caution if there is a salmonella problem in your area.

egg noodles also known as yellow noodles; made from wheat flour and eggs, sold fresh and dried. Range in size from very fine strands to wide, thick spaghetti-like pieces as thick as a shoelace.

eggplant also known as aubergine. May also be purchased char-grilled, packed in oil, in jars.

fennel also known as finocchio or anise. Also the name given to dried seeds having a licorice flavour. Eaten raw in salads or braised or fried as a vegetable accompaniment.

fillo pastry also known as phyllo; tissue-thin pastry sheets purchased chilled or frozen.

fish sauce also called nam pla or nuoc nam; made from pulverised salted fermented fish, most often anchovies. Has a pungent smell and strong taste; use sparingly.

five-spice powder a fragrant mixture of ground cinnamon, cloves, star anise, sichuan pepper and fennel seeds.

flour
plain: an all-purpose flour, made from wheat.
self-raising: plain flour sifted with baking powder in the proportion of 1 cup flour to 2 teaspoons baking powder.

Frangelico hazelnut-flavoured liqueur.

galangal also known as ka, a rhizome with a hot ginger-citrusy flavour; used similarly to ginger and garlic. Sometimes known as thai, siamese or laos ginger, it also comes in a dried powdered form called laos. Fresh ginger can be substituted for fresh galangal, but the flavour of the dish will not be the same.

garam masala a blend of spices, originating in North India; based on varying proportions of cardamom, cinnamon, cloves, coriander, fennel and cumin, roasted and ground together. Black pepper and chilli can be added for a hotter version.

hoisin sauce a thick, sweet and spicy chinese paste made from salted fermented soy beans, onions and garlic.

hokkien noodles also known as stir-fry noodles; fresh wheat noodles resembling thick, yellow-brown spaghetti needing no pre-cooking before being used.

instant noodles quick-cook noodles; also sold packaged as 2-minute noodles, with flavour sachet enclosed.

jam also known as preserve or conserve; most often made from fruit.

kaffir lime leaves also known as bai magrood, sold fresh, dried or frozen; looks like two glossy dark green leaves joined end to end, forming a rounded hourglass shape. Dried leaves are less potent, so double the number called for in a recipe if you substitute them for fresh leaves.

kecap manis also known as ketjap manis; dark, thick, sweet soy sauce used in most South-East Asian cooking. Depending on the brand, the soy's sweetness is derived from the addition of either molasses or palm sugar when brewed.

kumara Polynesian name of orange-fleshed sweet potato often confused with yam.

lavash flat, unleavened bread of Mediterranean origin.

lebanese cucumber long, slender and thin-skinned; this variety is also known as the european or burpless cucumber.

lemon grass tall, clumping, lemon-smelling and -tasting, sharp-edged grass; the white lower part of the stem is used, finely chopped, in cooking.

lentils (red, brown, yellow) dried pulses often identified by and named after their colour. Also known as dhal.

lettuce
cos: also known as romaine lettuce.
iceberg: a heavy, firm round lettuce with tightly packed leaves and crisp texture.
lamb's: also known as lamb's tongue, corn salad or mache, it has clusters of tiny, tender, nutty-tasting leaves.
radicchio: burgundy-leaved lettuce with white ribs and a slightly bitter flavour.

macadamia native to Australia, a rich and buttery nut; store in refrigerator because of high oil content.

Malibu coconut-flavoured rum.

marmalade a preserve, usually based on citrus fruit.

mayonnaise we prefer to use whole-egg mayonnaise in our recipes.

mesclun is a salad mix, or gourmet salad mix, with an assortment of young lettuce and other green leaves, including baby spinach leaves, mizuna and curly endive.

mexican seasoning mix a packaged seasoning meant to duplicate mexican flavours; made from oregano, cumin, chillies and other spices.

mince also known as ground, as in ground chicken, lamb, beef or pork.

mint, vietnamese not a mint at all, but a pungent and peppery narrow-leafed member of the buckwheat family. Not confined to Vietnam, it is also known as cambodian mint, pak pai (Thailand), laksa leaf (Indonesia), daun kesom (Singapore) and rau ram in Vietnam.

mirin a champagne-coloured, japanese cooking wine made of glutinous rice and alcohol, expressly for cooking and should not be confused with sake; there is a seasoned sweet mirin called manjo mirin that is made of water, rice, corn syrup and alcohol.

mushroom
button: small, cultivated white mushrooms with a mild flavour.
flat: large, flat mushrooms with a rich, earthy flavour, ideal for filling and barbecuing. They are sometimes misnamed field mushrooms, which are wild mushrooms.
shiitake: when fresh are also known as chinese black, forest or golden oak mushrooms; although cultivated, have the earthiness and taste of wild mushrooms. Are large and meaty; often used as a substitute for meat in some Asian-style vegetarian dishes. When dried, they are known as donko or dried chinese mushrooms; need to be rehydrated before use.
swiss brown: light to dark brown mushrooms with full-bodied flavour, also known as roman or cremini. Button or cap mushrooms can be substituted.

mussels should be bought from a fish market where there is reliably fresh fish. They must be tightly closed when bought, indicating they are alive. Before cooking, scrub the shells with a strong brush and remove the "beards". Discard any shells that do not open after cooking.

mustard
dijon: a pale brown, distinctively flavoured, fairly mild french mustard.
powder: finely ground white (yellow) mustard seeds.
wholegrain: also known as seeded mustard. A French-style coarse-grain mustard made from crushed mustard seeds and dijon-style french mustard.

oil
olive: made from ripened olives. Extra virgin and virgin are the best, while extra light or light refers to taste not fat levels.
peanut: pressed from ground peanuts; most commonly used oil in asian cooking because of its high smoke point (capacity to handle high heat without burning).
sesame: made from roasted, crushed, white sesame seeds; a flavouring rather than a cooking medium.
vegetable: any of a number of oils sourced from plants rather than animal fats.

onion
brown and white: are interchangeable. Their pungent flesh adds flavour to a vast range of dishes.
green: also known as scallion or, incorrectly, shallot; an immature onion picked before the bulb has formed, having a long, bright-green edible stalk.

red: also known as spanish, red spanish or bermuda onion; a sweet-flavoured, large purple-red onion.

orange flower water concentrated flavouring made from orange blossoms.

oyster sauce Asian in origin; a rich, brown sauce made from oysters and their brine, cooked with salt and soy sauce, and thickened with starches.

pancetta italian bacon that is cured, but not smoked.

paprika ground, dried red capsicum (bell pepper), available sweet or hot.

parsley, flat-leaf also known as continental parsley or italian parsley.

patty-pan squash also known as crookneck or custard marrow pumpkins; a round, slightly flat summer squash, yellow to pale green in colour and having a scalloped edge. Harvested young, it has firm white flesh and distinct flavour.

pide comes in long (about 45cm) flat loaves as well as individual rounds; made from wheat flour and sprinkled with sesame or black onion seeds.

pine nuts also known as pignoli; not, in fact, a nut, but a small, cream-coloured kernel from pine cones.

plum sauce a thick, sweet and sour dipping sauce made from plums, vinegar, sugar, chillies and spices.

polenta also known as cornmeal; flour-like cereal made of dried corn (maize) sold ground in different textures; also the name of the dish made from it.

prawns also known as shrimp.

puff pastry packaged sheets of frozen puff pastry, available from supermarkets.

redcurrant jelly a preserve made from redcurrants; used as a glaze for desserts and meats or in sauces.

red curry paste a combination of dried red chillies, onions, garlic, oil, lemon rind, shrimp paste, ground cumin, paprika, ground turmeric and ground black pepper.

rice
arborio: small, round-grain rice, well-suited to absorb a large amount of liquid; especially suitable for risottos.
basmati: a white, fragrant long-grained rice. It should be washed several times before cooking. Most usually associated with the food of India.
jasmine: fragrant long-grained rice; white rice can be substituted, but will not taste the same.

rice noodles, fresh also known as ho fun, khao pun, sen yau, pho or kway tiau, depending on the country of manufacture; the most common form of noodles used in Thailand; can be purchased in various widths or large sheets weighing about 500g, which are cut into the noodle width desired. Chewy and pure white, they do not need pre-cooking before use.

rice paper sheets also known as banh trang. Made from rice paste and stamped into rounds; stores well at room temperature. Are quite brittle and will break if dropped; dipped momentarily in water become pliable wrappers for fried food and uncooked vegetables. Make good spring-roll wrappers.

rice stick noodles also known as sen lek, ho fun or kway teow; come in different widths; dried noodles made from rice flour and water; available flat and wide or very thin (vermicelli). Should be soaked in boiling water to soften.

rice vermicelli also known as sen mee, mei fun or bee hoon. These are used throughout Asia in spring rolls and cold salads; similar to bean threads, only they're longer and made with rice flour instead of mung bean starch.

rocket also known as arugula, rugula and rucola; a peppery-tasting green leaf that can be used similarly to baby spinach leaves, eaten raw in salad or used in cooking. Baby rocket leaves are both smaller and less peppery.

rum we prefer to use an underproof rum (not overproof) for a more subtle flavour.

saffron threads stigma of a member of the crocus family, available in strands or ground form; imparts a yellow-orange colour to food once infused. Quality varies greatly; the best is the most expensive spice in the world. Should be stored in the freezer.

sage pungent herb with narrow, grey-green leaves; slightly bitter with a musty mint taste and aroma. Refrigerate fresh sage wrapped in a paper towel and sealed in a plastic bag for up to four days. Dried sage comes whole, rubbed (crumbled) and ground. It should be stored in a cool, dark place for no more than six months.

sake Japan's favourite rice wine; used either for drinking, or in cooking, marinating and as part of dipping sauces. If sake is unavailable, dry sherry, vermouth or brandy can be used as a substitute.

sambal oelek (also ulek or olek) Indonesian in origin; a salty paste made from ground chillies and vinegar.

satay sauce a traditional Indonesian and Malaysian-style spicy peanut sauce served with grilled meat skewers. Make your own, or buy one of the many packaged versions easily obtained from supermarkets or specialty Asian food stores.

savoy cabbage large, heavy head with crinkled dark-green outer leaves; a fairly mild-tasting cabbage.

sesame seeds black and white are the most common of this small oval seed, however, there are red and brown varieties also. A good source of calcium; used in cuisines the world over as an ingredient in cooking and as a condiment. To toast: spread seeds evenly on oven tray, toast in moderate oven briefly.

shrimp paste also known as kapi, trasi and blanchan; a strong-scented, very firm preserved paste made of salted, dried shrimp. Used as a pungent flavouring in many South-East Asian soups and sauces. It should be chopped or sliced thinly then wrapped in foil and roasted before use.

sichuan peppercorns also known as szechuan or chinese pepper, native to the Sichuan province of China. A mildly-hot spice that comes from the prickly ash tree. Although it is not related to the peppercorn family, small, red-brown aromatic sichuan berries look like black peppercorns, and have a distinctive peppery-lemon flavour and aroma.

snow peas also called mange tout ("eat all"). *tendrils:* the growing shoots of the plant; are sold by greengrocers.

soy sauce also known as sieu, is made from fermented soy beans. Several variations are available in most supermarkets and Asian food stores. We used a mild Japanese variety.

spinach also known as english spinach and, incorrectly, silverbeet.

squid is a type of mollusc; also known as calamari. Buy squid hoods to make preparation easier.

stock available in cans or tetra packs. Stock cubes or powder can be used. As a guide, 1 teaspoon of stock powder or 1 small crumbled stock cube mixed with 1 cup (250ml) water will give a fairly strong stock. Be aware of the salt and fat content of stock cubes and powders and prepared stocks.

sugar snap peas also known as honey snap peas; fresh small pea that can be eaten whole, pod and all, similarly to snow peas.

sugar we used coarse, granulated table sugar, also known as crystal sugar, unless otherwise specified.
brown: an extremely soft, fine granulated sugar retaining molasses for its characteristic colour and flavour.
caster: also known as superfine or finely granulated table sugar.
icing mixture: also known as confectioners' sugar or powdered sugar; granulated sugar crushed together with a small amount (about 3%) cornflour added.
palm: also known as nam tan pip, jaggery, jawa or gula melaka; made from the sap of the sugar palm tree. Light brown to black in colour and usually sold in rock-hard cakes; substitute it with brown sugar if unavailable.

sumac a purple-red, astringent spice ground from berries growing on shrubs that flourish wild around the Mediterranean; adds a tart, lemony flavour to dips and dressings and goes well with barbecued meat. Can be found in Middle-Eastern food stores. Substitute: ½ teaspoon lemon pepper + ⅛ teaspoon five spice + ⅛ teaspoon all spice = ¾ teaspoon sumac.

sweet chilli sauce the comparatively mild, thin thai sauce made from red chillies, sugar, garlic and vinegar; used as a condiment more often than in cooking.

Tabasco sauce brand name of an extremely fiery sauce made from vinegar, hot red peppers and salt.

tandoori paste consisting of garlic, tamarind, ginger, coriander, chilli and spices.

telegraph cucumber long and green with ridges running down its entire length; also known as continental cucumber.

teriyaki marinade a blend of soy sauce, wine, vinegar and spices.

teriyaki sauce usually made from a blend of soy sauce, mirin, sugar, ginger and other spices; it imparts a distinctive glaze when brushed on grilled meat.

tikka masala paste consisting of chilli, coriander, cumin, lentil flour, garlic, ginger, oil, turmeric, fennel, pepper, cloves, cinnamon and cardamom.

tofu also known as bean curd; an off-white, custard-like product made from the "milk" of crushed soy beans, comes as soft or firm. Leftover fresh tofu can be refrigerated in water (which is changed daily) up to four days. *fried:* packaged pieces of soft bean curd that has been deep-fried until the surface is brown and crusty and the inside almost dry.

tomato
paste: triple-concentrated tomato puree used to flavour soups, stews, sauces and casseroles.
puree: canned pureed tomatoes (not tomato paste). Substitute with fresh peeled and pureed tomatoes.
sun-dried: we used sun-dried tomatoes packaged in oil, unless otherwise specified.
sun-dried tomato pesto: a thick paste made from sun-dried tomatoes, oil, vinegar and herbs.

tortilla originally from Mexico, this thin, round unleavened bread can be made at home or purchased frozen, fresh or vacuum-packed. Two kinds are available, one made from wheat flour and the other from corn.

turmeric also known as kamin, is a rhizome related to galangal and ginger; must be grated or pounded to release its somewhat acrid aroma and pungent flavour. Known for

the golden colour it imparts to the dishes of which it's a part, fresh turmeric can be substituted with the more common dried powder (use 2 teaspoons of ground turmeric plus a teaspoon of sugar for every 20g of fresh turmeric called for in a recipe.)

thyme a member of the mint family, it has tiny grey-green leaves that give off a pungent minty, light-lemon aroma. Dried thyme comes in both leaf and powder form, and should be stored in a cool, dark place for no more than three months. Fresh thyme should be stored in the refrigerator, wrapped in a damp paper towel and placed in a sealed bag for no more than a few days.

vinegar
balsamic: authentic only from the province of Modena, Italy; made from a regional wine of white Trebbiano grapes specially processed then aged in antique wooden casks to give the exquisite pungent flavour.
cider: made from fermented apples.
red wine: based on fermented red wine.
rice: a colourless vinegar made from fermented rice and flavoured with sugar and salt. Also known as seasoned rice vinegar.
rice wine: made from rice wine lees (sediment left after fermentation), salt and alcohol.
tarragon: white wine vinegar infused with fresh tarragon.
white: made from spirit of cane sugar.

wasabi an asian horseradish used to make the pungent, green-coloured sauce traditionally served with Japanese raw fish dishes; sold in powdered or paste form.

water chestnuts resembles a chestnut in appearance, hence the English name. They are small brown tubers with a crisp, white, nutty-tasting flesh. Their crunchy texture is best experienced fresh, however, canned water chestnuts are more easily obtained and can be kept about a month, once opened, under refrigeration.

watercress one of the cress family, a large group of peppery greens used raw in salads, dips and sandwiches, or cooked in soups. Highly perishable, so must be used as soon as possible after purchase.

witlof also known as chicory or belgian endive; cigar-shaped, tightly packed heads with pale, yellow-green tips. Has a delicately bitter flavour. May be cooked or eaten raw.

worcestershire sauce a thin, dark-brown spicy sauce used as a seasoning for meat, gravies and cocktails, and as a condiment.

yogurt we used plain, unflavoured yogurt, unless otherwise specified.

zucchini also known as courgette.

index

facts and figures

Wherever you live, you'll be able to use our recipes with the help of these easy-to-follow conversions. While these conversions are approximate only, the difference between an exact and the approximate conversion of various liquid and dry measures is but minimal and will not affect your cooking results.

dry measures

metric	imperial
15g	1/2 oz
30g	1oz
60g	2oz
90g	3oz
125g	4oz (1/4lb)
155g	5oz
185g	6oz
220g	7oz
250g	8oz (1/2lb)
280g	9oz
315g	10oz
345g	11oz
375g	12oz (3/4lb)
410g	13oz
440g	14oz
470g	15oz
500g	16oz (1lb)
750g	24oz (11/2lb)
1kg	32oz (2lb)

liquid measures

metric	imperial
30ml	1 fluid oz
60ml	2 fluid oz
100ml	3 fluid oz
125ml	4 fluid oz
150ml	5 fluid oz (1/4 pint/1 gill)
190ml	6 fluid oz
250ml	8 fluid oz
300ml	10 fluid oz (1/2 pint)
500ml	16 fluid oz
600ml	20 fluid oz (1 pint)
1000ml (1 litre)	1 3/4 pints

helpful measures

metric	imperial
3mm	1/8in
6mm	1/4in
1cm	1/2in
2cm	3/4in
2.5cm	1in
5cm	2in
6cm	2 1/2in
8cm	3in
10cm	4in
13cm	5in
15cm	6in
18cm	7in
20cm	8in
23cm	9in
25cm	10in
28cm	11in
30cm	12in (1ft)

measuring equipment

The difference between one country's measuring cups and another's is, at most, within a 2 or 3 teaspoon variance. (For the record, one Australian metric measuring cup holds approximately 250ml.) The most accurate way of measuring dry ingredients is to weigh them. When measuring liquids, use a clear glass or plastic jug with metric markings. (One Australian metric tablespoon holds 20ml; one Australian metric teaspoon holds 5ml.)

Note: North America, NZ and the UK use 15ml tablespoons. All cup and spoon measurements are level. We use large eggs having an average weight of 60g.

how to measure

When using graduated metric measuring cups, shake dry ingredients loosely into the appropriate cup. Do not tap the cup on a bench or tightly pack the ingredients unless directed to do so. Level top of measuring cups and measuring spoons with a knife. When measuring liquids, place a clear glass or plastic jug with metric markings on a flat surface to check accuracy at eye level.

oven temperatures

These oven temperatures are only a guide. Always check the manufacturer's manual.

	°C (Celsius)	°F (Fahrenheit)	Gas Mark
Very slow	120	250	1
Slow	150	300	2
Moderately slow	160	325	3
Moderate	180 – 190	350 – 375	4
Moderately hot	200 – 210	400 – 425	5
Hot	220 – 230	450 – 475	6
Very hot	240 – 250	500 – 525	7

Senior editor *Wendy Bryant*
Designer *Alison Windmill*
Food editor *Louise Patniotis*
Special feature photographer *Andre Martin*
Special feature stylist *Jane Hann*
Special feature home economist *Susie Riggall*
Food director *Pamela Clark*
Nutritional information *Laila Ibram*

ACP Books Staff
Editorial director *Susan Tomnay*
Creative director *Hieu Chi Nguyen*
Editorial coordinator *Caroline Lowry*
Editorial assistant *Karen Lai*
Publishing manager (sales) *Brian Cearnes*
Publishing manager (rights & new projects) *Jane Hazell*
Brand manager *Donna Gianniotis*
Pre-press *Harry Palmer*
Production manager *Carol Currie*
Business manager *Seymour Cohen*
Assistant business analyst *Martin Howes*
Chief executive officer *John Alexander*
Group publisher *Pat Ingram*
Publisher *Sue Wannan*

Produced by ACP books, Sydney.
Printing by SNP Leefung Printers Limited, China.
Published by ACP Publishing Pty Limited,
54 Park St, Sydney; GPO Box 4088, Sydney, NSW 1028.
Ph: (02) 9282 8618 Fax: (02) 9267 9438.
acpbooks@acp.com.au
www.acpbooks.com.au

To order books phone 136 116.
Send recipe enquiries to
recipeenquiries@acp.com.au

AUSTRALIA: Distributed by Network Services,
GPO Box 4088, Sydney, NSW 1028.
Ph: (02) 9282 8777 Fax: (02) 9264 3278.
UNITED KINGDOM: Distributed by Australian Consolidated
Press (UK), Moulton Park Business Centre, Red House Rd,
Moulton Park, Northampton, NN3 6AQ
Ph: (01604) 497 531 Fax: (01604) 497 533 acpukltd@aol.com
CANADA: Distributed by Whitecap Books Ltd, 351 Lynn Ave.
North Vancouver, BC. V7J 2C4
Ph: (604) 980 9852 Fax: (604) 980 8197
customerservice@whitecap.ca www.whitecap.ca
NEW ZEALAND: Distributed by Netlink Distribution Company,
Level 4, 23 Hargreaves St, College Hill, Auckland 1,
Ph: (9) 302 7616.

Clark, Pamela.
Great Fast Recipes.

Includes index.
ISBN 1 86396 338 3

1.Quick and easy cookery. I. Title. II Title: Great Fast Recipes
III. Title: Australian Women's Weekly.
641.555

© ACP Publishing Pty Limited 2004
ABN 18 053 273 546

Photographers: Alan Benson, Steve Brown, Robert Clark,
Brett Danton, Ben Dearnley, Joe Filshie, Rowan Fotheringham,
Ian Hofstetter, Louise Lister, Ashley Mackevicius, Andre Martin,
Mark O'Meara, Rob Shaw, Brett Stevens, Robert Taylor, Ian Wallace.

Stylists: Wendy Berecry, Julz Beresford, Janelle Bloom,
Marie-Helene Clauzon, Jane Hann, Mary Harris, Katy Holder,
Amber Kelly, Sarah O'Brien, Louise Pickford, Suzie Smith, Sophia Young.

Cover: Scallops with snow peas and noodles, page 155
Photographer: Andre Martin
Stylist: Jane Hann

Back cover: ice-cream sundae with berry sauce
and almond wafers, page 238
Photographer: Ben Dearnley
Stylist: Janelle Bloom